Evangelism: A Road Less Traveled

BY GENE R. SIMOWITZ

Copyright © 2012 by Gene R. Simowitz

EVANGELISM: A Road Less Traveled
by Gene R. Simowitz

Printed in the United States of America

ISBN 9781619966321

All rights reserved solely by the author. The author guarantees all contents are original and do not infringe upon the legal rights of any other person or work. No part of this book may be reproduced in any form without the permission of the author. The views expressed in this book are not necessarily those of the publisher.

Unless otherwise stated, all Scripture quotations are taken from the New International Version of the Bible, copyrighted © 1973, 1978, 1984 by International Bible Society.

www.xulonpress.com

DEDICATION

With so many people to thank for the conception of this initial book, it's literally impossible to single out any one individual for this dedication. So, I must ask the reader's indulgence as I narrow it down to just the barest minimum of those to whom I owe a great debt of gratitude.

To my son, David, who ignited the spark that brought to full burn the flame of this idea which had been smoldering deep inside my heart for several months.

To my son, Luke, who continued to fan that flame by unceasingly encouraging me with his insightful, thoughtful and thought-provoking motivational words and suggestions.

To my sister, Jo, who has seen me at my worst as well as my best all my life, and still loved and supported me through it all.

To my father, Anthony Simowitz, a lover of souls and evangelism, who indeed had the mind of Christ, and who set my feet on the straight and narrow path early on in life, who never stopped praying for his wayward son, even after his feet were firmly planted on that path, and of whom it could be said without hesitation, "He pointed others to Jesus."

To Bob Randall, my pastor, mentor, father in the ministry, and evangelist in his own right. He was my apostle Paul; I was his Timothy. He gave me my first taste of soul winning and evangelism, and taught me what it means to "do the work of an evangelist."

To Delos Miles, my evangelism professor, whose burning love for lost souls was undeniable, who lived and modeled evangelism the way he taught it, and who showed me that, although it is hard work, evangelism can also be one of the most exciting and rewarding opportunities for the Christian, and we should seize everyone of them.

Contents

Foreword	ix
Introduction	xiii
1. Evangelism As A Priority	21
2. Being A Friend	40
3. The Road To Becoming A Friend	56
4. Evangelism's Battle With Goodness	69
5. Apathy: A Major Bump In The Road	92
6. Miss The Sign…Miss Your Turn	110
7. The Importance Of Being A Flagger *(EDWARD KIMBALL)*	128
8. Be On The Lookout For Blind Spots *(THOMAS)*	151
9. Beware The Paralysis Of Traffic Jams *(ELIZABETH)*	170
10. No Dead Ends On *This* Road	190
11. No U-turns Allowed *(EDDIE)*	205
12. Road Under Construction	228
13. Shortcuts Can Be Costly	241
14. The Importance Of The Hidden Entrance *(THE INVISIBLE WOMAN) (THE OLD MISSIONARY)*	258

15. Evangelism: A Road That Never Ends   **275**
(LITTLE OLD WHITE-HAIRED MAN)

Afterword   **303**

Witnessing Helps   **307**

FOREWORD

The motif used to present to the reader this study in evangelism is one of traveling down a road. As Christians, we are just "passing through" this life here on earth. There will be many of life's different roads we will travel before we reach our ultimate destination in heaven. But because of Christ's command given us in Matthew 28:18-20, which we all know as the Great Commission, the one road we will continually be traveling is this road of evangelism. Although the chapters are intended to flow together into a unity, they may also stand alone. Because all evangelism is telling the Good News regardless of what method is used, there is some intentional repetition and overlapping of content.

Although I was already twenty-seven years old when I became a Christian, almost immediately I developed a love for evangelism. Initially, it was because of the incredible feeling of inner cleansing and God's love and forgiveness I experienced upon my conversion in May, 1975, and I wanted everyone who had not already done so, to experience that same wonderful feeling that I had experienced. But that love for evangelism is also due in part to the influence of three remarkable Christians who had a great impact on my Christian life. One was my own father, who was also a Baptist pastor and had a burning love for, and a desire to see, lost souls come to know Jesus as their Savior. The second person was my own pastor and mentor in Wichita, Kansas, Bob Randall, who not only was a loving and sensitive pastor-teacher, but also an outstanding evangelist in his own right. The third individual was my professor of evangelism in seminary, Delos Miles, who harbored a deep, unmistakable, and obvious love for lost persons, and who showed his students how exciting and rewarding evangelism really can be.

Throughout this book, you will readily see that I take evangelism very seriously. One of my goals is to present this idea of evangelism and its importance in such a way that any lay Christian who is serious about obeying Christ's command can see the importance of it. But this volume is also addressed to pastors and other church staff members who may need help in trying to encourage their congregation to embrace as their own this Great Commission of our Lord, and be willing to obey His marching orders. If we are to be obedient to Him we have no choice here, because it is my conviction that each generation of Christians is responsible for evangelizing the lost of their own generation.

Jesus was an evangelist par excellence. He was an evangelist without a peer. He knew what made persons tick. If we wish to learn how to win the lost to Christ, we need to study His methods with them. If we major on anything in our evangelism, let it be the imitation of Christ.

With each biblical illustration used in these chapters I have made reference to various passages of Scripture. Although these Scripture passages may be familiar to the reader, I encourage you to read the respective verses relating to each incident, as I feel those who do read them will have a more enlightening ride, and more clearly grasp the issues the author is trying to address. With that being said, I hope that as you read, you will have an open Bible at hand.

I have often felt that it takes God longer to get a Christian ready to witness than it takes Him to get a lost person ready to be saved; and if by reading the following pages may in some way cause you to realize the importance of evangelism and encourages you to get off the sidelines and get involved, then this book has served its intended purpose. As a means of helping those who are unsure how to approach a witnessing interview, or what Scripture passages may be useful, I have included at the back of this book a few "helps" which I hope will ease some of your trepidation.

A final word about the conception of this book. I had been tossing around in my head the idea of writing a book for a couple of months. I was sitting at a picnic table with my oldest son, David, and his wife, and my two grandsons, at the annual Sharptown Carnival, in Sharptown, Maryland, enjoying some delicious fried oyster sandwiches (no one makes fried oyster sandwiches like those wonderful ladies at the Sharptown Carnival), when all of a sudden David remarked, "Dad, you oughta write a book. You could write one on evangelism." Thus began my own journey down this new road in my life, which has been paved with much joy, love, prayer, and gratitude to God that He has given me this opportunity to share with you insights from my heart.

EVANGELISM: A ROAD LESS TRAVELED

INTRODUCTION

What is evangelism? It goes without saying that there have been numerous—perhaps it would be safe to say almost countless—numbers of books written about this most important subject. Not to say that this is the most important subject in Christianity. But in order for us as Christians to fulfill the Great Commission Jesus gave His disciples—and to us—as He ascended into heaven, it behooves us to seriously take up this challenge issued to us by the Son of God. Let's face it. If God did not have a work for us to do, first of all, He would not have left the disciples behind with this command; and secondly, He would not leave us here on the earth once we become Christians. God has a work for us to do.

Jesus commanded us to go into all the world and proclaim the good news of the gospel, to reach as many souls for Jesus Christ as we possibly can. In order for us to do that, we must be evangelists. No, not in the "professional" sense of the word, as is the common thought most people have when they hear the term, "evangelist," such as Billy Graham and others like him. But, rather, we are to be evangelists based upon the biblical definition of the word.

The word, "evangelism" comes from the Greek word, "euaggelion," which actually means "good news" or "good tidings." So, from the biblical point of view an "evangelist" is a person who simply tells forth the "good news" of the gospel of Jesus Christ. Yes, the apostle Paul does mention in Ephesians 4:11-12, that God did indeed give some to be evangelists along with others who were given the gift of apostles, prophets, pastors and teachers; and, yes, those are specific offices to which God has called certain people. But for our purpose here in this discussion, we will be referring to simply the Greek definition of evangelism.

Jesus said to go into all the world. I think of the parable Jesus told in Matthew 20:1-16, about the landowner who sent laborers to go work in his vineyard. The world all around us is God's vineyard. As Christians, we are all laborers in His vineyard, and with millions of souls lost and dying in their sin without Jesus Christ as their Savior, there is more than enough work to keep us busy, whether we start working at the beginning of the day, the middle of the day, or near the end of the day. Whether we begin witnessing to others about Jesus Christ early in our Christian lives or later on, there will always be enough lost souls who need to hear the good news of Jesus' love for them. The Lord is in the business of bringing people into His family by using imperfect human beings like you and I in order to introduce them to the only Person, Jesus Christ, who can bring them hope and happiness and peace, not only in this life, but in the life to come.

The world into which Jesus sends us is all around us. It could be that next door neighbor, the grocery clerk, your hair stylist, the mechanic who changes your car's oil every three or four thousand miles, a coworker, a family member, a fellow passenger on an airplane, the partner with whom you exercise every day, or even that person you see every Sunday in church whom you assume may already be a Christian. The point being, of course, that evangelism is everywhere we look, if we just open our eyes and open our hearts to the leading of God's Holy Spirit.

My evangelism professor in seminary, Dr. Delos Miles, stated on the first day of class that God is not so much interested in our *ability* as He is in our *availability*. He went on to say that contrary to what we hear so often, evangelism is not necessarily anywhere we find it, but, rather it is anywhere we *want* to find it. Are we making ourselves available to God's Holy Spirit to lead us to that one particular person He wants us to tell about Jesus at that one particular moment in their lives and in ours? We don't know that maybe, just maybe, God has placed us at that specific place at that specific time to share Jesus with that specific person, because that may have been the only chance that person would have ever had to hear about the good news of the saving power of Jesus Christ.

So, then, with all of that being said—truths that most of us probably already know—why another book on evangelism? Why venture into the same area of discussion where so many other esteemed and admired biblical scholars—writers far more gifted and knowledgeable than I—have already gone?

I would like to clarify right from the beginning that this is not an attempt to put forth a quick, easy-as-one-two-three, approach to evangelizing the world and soul-winning. Although I must say that telling forth the good news of Jesus Christ may not be as difficult as many people feel that it is. As Christians, we all have a story to tell. In my own personal experience, and from hearing the testimony of other Christians, I truly believe that once we begin to take this business of evangelism seriously, and begin to sincerely witness to others of their need for Jesus, and see souls come to the Lord Jesus Christ through salvation, it will become almost addictive. The joy and excitement we experience, and the gratitude we feel because God chose to use *us* in His great plan for mankind, will be such that we won't want to stop, and we will, indeed, begin to realize that evangelism *is* "anywhere we *want* to find it."

Although we will be traveling over very familiar ground within the next several pages, perhaps there may be just one or two ideas or thoughts which will jump off the page and grab your attention—something you never realized or saw before. Or perhaps as you read, maybe you will be encouraged to start out on this path of proclaiming the good tidings of Jesus' love. Or it could be that after you have finished reading, a spark will be ignited that will rekindle that evangelistic fire that used to burn so hotly inside of you, but for one reason or another you have allowed it to burn low, almost to the point of being extinguished altogether.

I would often tell those who listened to my sermons, as I'm sure most preachers do, that even though they may have heard the message before, and even though the subject matter is very familiar to them, if they get just one thing out of the message that they can use to make them a better and stronger Christian, then as far as I'm concerned, the message has served its purpose. But by the same token, even if there wasn't anything that struck them as significant at that particular time, it still should not be considered a waste of their time, and as a preacher, I should not consider it a wasted effort as far as that particular person is concerned. The reason being that even though God's Holy Spirit did not speak to an individual's heart at that moment, who knows that somewhere farther down the road in God's perfect timing, He won't bring back to that person's mind something from that message which *will* play a significant role in that individual's life? It's like reading the Bible. It's happened to all of us I'm sure. We can read the same passage of scripture several times, and each time we read it, God may allow us to see something there that we did not see before. It just depends upon where we are at that particular moment in our walk with the Lord.

So, in answer to our question, I guess that's the bottom line. This is the reason why another book on evangelism. As we take this journey together, my prayer is that both the writer and the reader will receive some new insight into God's task for Christians—some new "something"— which will help sustain the flame that God wants burning in the hearts of all His people.

But to get back to our original question. What is evangelism? Well, once more I must refer to my evangelism professor, Delos Miles, who I feel developed what I have always believed to be the most comprehensive, all-encompassing, yet at the same time, concise definition for evangelism. He stated, *"Evangelism is being, doing, and telling the gospel of the Kingdom of God by the power of the Holy Spirit, in order to convert persons and structures to the lordship of Jesus Christ."* As we travel this road together, by using biblical and real-life examples, we will be exploring every avenue of that definition to see how all-encompassing it really is.

Enjoy the ride.

God bless you always and in all ways.

CHAPTER 1

EVANGELISM AS A PRIORITY

Evangelism: *"Being, doing, and telling the gospel of the Kingdom of God by the power of the Holy Spirit, in order to convert persons and structures to the Lordship of Jesus Christ."*

At the time I attended Midwestern Baptist Theological Seminary in Kansas City, Missouri, the semester schedule was referred to as "mini-mesters." As is usually the case in seminaries, our school weeks ran Tuesday through Friday, with no classes on Mondays. Unlike the typical semester in graduate and post graduate education, the mini-mesters were either four weeks long or eight weeks long. We didn't attend class one, two, or even three days a week. We were in class every day. If a particular course of study lasted four weeks, we were in class two hours each day. If it were an eight-week course, we were in class one hour each day. With the courses being encapsulated in such a manner, we received as much classroom time in four or eight weeks as the normal semester in other institutions which ran for four or five months at a time. For the most part, that really was not too bad of a schedule. I think, after a while, most of us came to the point where we actually liked the shortened schedule. We only really started feeling the pressure when it came time to finishing three, four, or maybe five term papers within a month's time, which was especially difficult when you consider most of us were also holding down a part time job to help pay for our seminary education.

Now, you may ask, "What in the world does all of that have to do with evangelism?" Nothing really, I suppose. But I mentioned that little bit of background history for a significant reason.

If my memory serves me correctly, my initial course in evangelism was one of those four-week courses. After the usual opening introductory remarks about the course, and discussing the course syllabus, the professor asked the question, "What is evangelism?" After hearing the various answers which were offered, Dr. Miles turned and wrote on the blackboard the definition above. When he finished writing, he turned back to the class and launched into a complete and thorough—almost word-by-word—exegesis of that definition, which took all the rest of the week, two hours every day until he finished with the word, "Christ." And when he was done many of us, I'm sure, felt there was still much more that could have been said.

I took on an entirely new appreciation of this thing we call "evangelism." From that moment on, I realized that if you let it, evangelism—soul-winning, reaching those people in need of Christ, seeing lives transformed by the power of God's Holy Spirit, watching souls snatched from the vise-like grip of Satan like brands plucked from the burning—can be one of the most exciting, rewarding, and awesome experiences you will ever have, if you will just allow the Holy Spirit to work in and through you. But, my friends, *that* is the key. In our own strength, in our own ability, in our own power we can never accomplish this Great Commission that Christ has laid out before us.

During His earthly ministry, Jesus left us with many great teachings and lessons which were handed down, first of all, by word of mouth from His disciples, and eventually through His Word, the Bible. But when He ascended back into heaven to be with His Father, He left us with one command only: To go into all the world and be His witnesses. As we study the life and ministry of Jesus, we see that He is not commanding us to do anything that He was not willing to, and did not, do Himself. Jesus was the ideal evangelist. It was a priority in His life, and He expects it to be a priority in our lives.

Before we go any farther in our study, however, I feel it would be a grave injustice if we did not at least spend a little time discussing our definition of evangelism. Naturally, we will not do an exhaustive study of it as was done in the classroom. But I believe we need to briefly hit the high points of what is being said here in order to appreciate the importance and seriousness of reaching out to others to spread the good news of the saving power of Jesus Christ.

Once again, evangelism is *"Being, doing, and telling the gospel of the Kingdom of God by the power of the Holy Spirit in order to convert persons and structures to the Lordship of Jesus Christ."*

Being the gospel of the Kingdom of God. One may ask, "How is that possible?" I'm certain that all of us at one time or another have heard that familiar statement, "To some people you may be the only Bible they will ever read." Did you catch that? You may *be* the only Bible.

I'm sure all of us have known Christians who, when we look at them, there just seems to be something "different" about them. They seem to have a certain appearance to their faces. There seems to be a certain quality of peace and even joy about them. Certainly, they have struggles, heartaches, and difficulties the same as the rest of us. But they just seem to bear up under the pressure much easier than so many others. If asked, they would very likely say something like, "It's just the joy of the Lord within me. I just draw on His strength and grace during those troublesome times in my life." What they're saying, in effect, is that they have experienced the good news of the saving power of Jesus Christ in their lives, and they are allowing that good news and all its fringe benefits to be manifested in their everyday lives. That's what we call *"being"* the gospel (the good news) of the Kingdom of God.

Perhaps we know of instances when a person has come to the saving knowledge of Christ not so much by what another individual said, as by how that individual acted during times of testing—people who have said they came to Christ, "not because of what he or she said or didn't say, but simply because of who they *were*." I remember a man named Eddie who had been fighting terminal cancer and because of the way he faced his ordeal head-on, a chain reaction was set in motion which resulted in numerous souls coming to know Jesus Christ as their personal savior. What an awesome legacy he left behind. More about Eddie later. (Don't spoil the fun by reading ahead to see how his story turned out. We have some groundwork to cover before then). Well, I suppose I can't really stop you if you choose to do so.

After Peter and John had testified before the Sanhedrin, that august religious group of Jewish leaders (the "preachers" of the day, if you will), we read in Acts 4:13, *"When they saw the courage of Peter and John and realized that they were unschooled, ordinary men, they were astonished and they took note that these men had been with Jesus."* Yes, of course, the words spoken by Peter and John were significant, but the religious leaders looked upon these men as *"unschooled"* and *"ordinary."* These men were not doctors or lawyers or educated men with seminary training. These were just plain, common fishermen. But the difference was that these men *"had been with Jesus,"* and that made all the difference in the world. That's what made these men who they were. Not all the lessons and teachings they had heard from the Master, although, of course, all of that was important, but the fact that they had been…with…Jesus.

Folks, when we spend serious, quality time with Jesus, it is going to affect every part of our being. Everything about us is going to change. Our look, our demeanor, our walk, our talk, our habits, our likes and dislikes, and the way we approach life in general, are all going to be transformed. Once we allow Jesus to take full control of our lives, we can never be the person we once were. Who we *are* is crucial in evangelism.

Doing the gospel of the Kingdom of God. How does one *do* the good news of Jesus Christ? We read that Jesus went about doing good. When we reach out to those in need in the name of Jesus, we are doing evangelism. That need may be major or minor…if there is such a thing as a minor need when it comes to Jesus in our lives. We never know how some little act, we think nothing of, may possibly affect someone else in a positive way. That one "insignificant" act may be just the catalyst needed to spur someone else on to finding salvation for his or her soul. Perhaps not right at that moment, but a seed could very likely have been planted which will ignite a spark that will eventually turn into a fire for Jesus that will burn hotly for Him.

We are familiar with the parable Jesus told in Matthew 25 about the sheep and the goats when He explains the importance of how the King had been hungry, thirsty, sick, unclothed, and a stranger, and the righteous tended to His needs. In the parable, when asked by the righteous when they had done all these things, Jesus replied, "Whatever you did for one of the least of these brothers of mine, you did for me" (vs. 40).

We should never underestimate the importance that what we *do* for others may be the difference between eternity with Jesus and eternity without Him.

Telling the gospel of the Kingdom of God. It almost seems this needs no explanation. It's pretty obvious what is meant by "telling." However, perhaps we need to spend a moment discussing just *how* we are doing that telling. There are so many, many approaches to witnessing and sharing the gospel with others, and I don't believe any of us can say any one method is *the* best or *the* most effective. I think it all depends on the circumstances and the situation at any given time. There are a countless number of Scripture verses we can turn to as well. But, once again, what works well with one person at a particular time may not necessarily work as well with someone else.

We have all heard that John 3:16 is the Gospel in a nutshell. I would have to agree. Whether a person is just starting down the road to witnessing or has been traveling it for years, that one little verse is still one of the most reliable verses to turn to when explaining to someone the need of salvation simply because it answers four very basic, important questions: 1. How does God feel about me? 2. What did Christ do for me? 3. What am I to do? 4. What is God's gift to me? It's simple, concise, and to the point.

Oftentimes, people will say, "When it comes to testifying about Jesus, I wouldn't know what to say. I'm afraid I'd just blow it and sound stupid. I'd be too nervous. What would I say?" My immediate reply has always been, "Just tell them what Jesus has done for *you*."

In one of my previous churches I often asked individuals to come up to the platform and give their testimony for Jesus in front of the church. No pressure was ever applied. It was all voluntary. If they agreed that was fine, but if they didn't that was fine too. As you may well imagine, there were some who immediately balked for the obvious reasons, some, of course, being not knowing what to say, or they couldn't speak in front of people. I understood and respected that. But before I took "no" as their final answer, I would give them four simple little statements to look over, which would form the basis of their testimony. Whether they were long-time veterans in the Christian army or just new recruits, I gave them all the same four statements. These four statements are pulled from the apostle Paul's testimony before King Agrippa in Acts 26:4-22. These nineteen verses can be read slowly and carefully in about three minutes, which is about as long as any typical testimony should be, if one does not elaborate a lot on the details. The four statements form the foundation of, and is essentially the crux of *every* person's testimony.

1. My life before receiving Christ (vv. 4-11).
2. How I realized I needed Christ (vv. 12-14).
3. How I became a Christian (vv.15-18).
4. How Christ helps me in my daily life (vs. 22).

In a courtroom trial, witnesses are often called to testify. We need to remember that the only purpose of a witness is to just tell what happened in his or her own words. As Joe Friday used to say on the TV series, "Dragnet," "Just the facts, ma'am." That's all God wants us to do. Just tell what happened. I remember someone asking me years ago, "How can you be *sure* you were saved?" I just looked at him and simply said, "Because I was there when it happened."

As we study Jesus' method of communicating, we find some important fundamental advice: Make it clear. Make it simple. Emphasize the essentials. Forget about impressing others. Be content to leave some things unsaid.

How we *tell* the Good News can make all the difference in the world.

The *gospel* of the Kingdom of God. As we have mentioned, "gospel" means "good news." The Bible contains both bad news and good news. The bad news is that all of us are sinners (Romans 3:23), and that the penalty for sin is death (Romans. 6:23). The good news is that Christ died for us (Romans 5:8). Therefore, we can be saved through faith in Him (Ephesians 2:8-9).

There is more than enough bad news in this world, and the last thing we want to hear is more of the same. Our task in evangelism is to let others know there is *good* news waiting to be heard.

Despite the difficulties and the hardships so many face; despite the pain and heartache, the suffering and loss so many experience, believe it or not, there is hope. Not everyone will accept our message of hope and salvation. But for those who do, the good news of the Kingdom of God will open doors for them that they never dreamed existed.

I really like the words of one of my favorite songs, *"Give Them All To Jesus,"* that the gospel singer, Evie Tornquist, would sing several years ago when it was one of the most popular contemporary Christian songs at that time:

> *"He never said we'd only see sunshine.*
> *"He never said there'd be no rain.*
> *"He only promised us a heart full of singing*
> *"At the very things that once brought pain."*

We have good news to share with people. We have good news that, yes, life will be difficult at times, but through it all, there is a person, Jesus, who can put a song in our hearts in the midst of the fieriest arrows hell may shoot at us. That is why observers were amazed at the sight of early Christian martyrs singing as they were being led to their deaths, to be devoured by hungry, ravenous beasts in the Roman coliseum. What made the difference? Only one thing. Jesus made the difference. Paul knew what he was talking about in Romans 8:18, when he was speaking not only for himself, but for all Christians everywhere in years to come as he wrote, *"I consider that our present sufferings are not worth comparing with the glory that will be revealed in us."*

The gospel of the *Kingdom of God*. As Christians, we know we all belong to the family of God. But when we become part of His family, we are also brought into His kingdom. This is not some earthly kingdom which will pass away eventually. This is not some temporary kingdom ruled by mortal man. This is the kingdom of the almighty, sovereign God. In 1 Peter 2:4-10, the apostle Peter writes about the priesthood of all believers and about Christians being a chosen people. But for the sake of our discussion here there is one word in verse 9 which stands out to me. Peter talks about our being a *royal* priesthood. God is telling us through Peter that He considers us *royalty*. As children of God, not only have we been brought into His kingdom, not only do we participate in all the benefits of His kingdom, but as a *royal* priesthood we serve Him, yes, but we will also *reign* with Him…alongside of Him. How much better could it get?

The Kingdom of God is a vast kingdom ruled by the sovereign Lord. When we invite others into this kingdom, we are asking them to swear allegiance to a King who will never be dethroned and to become subjects of a Kingdom which will never be overthrown.

By the *power of the Holy Spirit*. We are frail, weak, bumbling, stumbling mortal beings. And yet God has chosen *us* to advance His cause. God tells us in Zechariah 4:6: *"'Not by might nor by power, but by my Spirit,' says the Lord Almighty."* In our own strength and power we are helpless to further the kingdom of God. Even though God chooses to use us blundering human beings, He has given us a power unspeakable that will strengthen us and give us courage to do what we normally would be unable to do, and would probably bungle it, anyway, relying on our own ability.

Jesus promised us in John 14:12, *"I tell you the truth, anyone who has faith in me will do what I have been doing."* Jesus is promising us that because He sent His Holy Spirit to guide and empower us, we, too, can be witnesses to the love of God in Christ Jesus.

The apostle Paul tells us in Romans 8:17, that we are *"heirs of God, and joint heirs with Christ"* (KJV). What Paul is saying is that because we are *joint heirs* with Christ, all that belongs to Him belongs to us. So the same Holy Spirit, who was there for Him during His earthly ministry, is also here to help us today. That means we don't have to rely on our own strength and ability when it comes to sharing with others the good news of the Kingdom of God. God's Holy Spirit will move us along in His work just as He did in the life of Jesus and His disciples and the thousands of Christians since.

But there is another thing we need to understand about God's Holy Spirit. We need to remember it is the Spirit who does the convicting, and it is Jesus who does the saving. Our task is to just bear witness. As we mentioned earlier, not everyone will receive our message. If we have been faithful in our work as evangelists, if we have been true to the Word, if we have relied on God's Holy Spirit to lead us, if we have faithfully proclaimed the good news, then we should not consider our mission a failure if an individual refuses our message. Even Jesus saw people walk away from Him. We are to be faithful in our calling and leave the rest up to God.

In order to convert persons and structures. We know that "convert" simply means to change. Once again, we must remember we are to testify to the saving power of Jesus Christ with the hope that the Holy Spirit will move and convict the people to whom we are speaking, and cause them to change their life's direction. That's what repentance is. A person is heading in one direction and then makes a 180-degree turn and goes in the opposite direction. We want to see that person make a complete about face and change his or her way of thinking, acting, talking, and living. We are praying for a change in habits and lifestyle

"But," you may ask, "What is meant by the term, *structures?*"

When we think of that term, we are immediately reminded of physical edifices, such as buildings, houses, mansions, towers, etc. But we have to remember that that term is also used when referring to the family structure. The Bible brings out incidents when entire families came to salvation through the witness of one of God's servants.

In Acts 10:23-48, we read about how Peter went to the home of Cornelius after having a vision God had sent him. We're all familiar with the story how after preaching to the household of Cornelius, his entire family and friends received Christ and were baptized.

We are also familiar with the experience of Paul and Silas in Acts 16:25-34, when they were imprisoned in Philippi. We remember how an angel shook the foundations of the prison, and when the jailer saw the prison doors open, he was about to kill himself when Paul and Silas stopped him. The jailer asked what he must do to be saved. Paul and Silas told him, *"Believe in the Lord Jesus, and you will be saved—you and your household"* (vs. 31). Afterwards, the jailer took them to his house and we read that the jailer *"was filled with joy because he had come to believe in God—he and his whole family"* (vs. 34).

I have seen, as I'm sure many others have seen, how the conversion of just one family member can influence the rest of the family so much so that every member of that family comes to know the Lord Jesus Christ as their savior.

How do we know that by sharing the good news with just one person will not in turn bring about a complete change not only in that one person's life, but also in the lives of his family and his structure of friends? It doesn't *always* happen that way, but sometimes it does.

In order to convert persons and structures to the *Lordship of Jesus Christ*. When we become a Christian that is only the beginning. It is like a series of messages I heard a pastor preach one time. The series was entitled, *"Event vs. Process."*

We have had a salvation experience with Jesus Christ. That was the event. Now the process begins. For us to make it through each day of our lives with all the numerous setbacks we may experience—the disappointments, the heartaches, the sufferings, the losses such as loved ones, jobs, income, crises such as sickness or betrayal or divorce—we need an inner strength upon which to draw. Remember the fourth statement in our testimony? *"How Christ helps me in my daily life."* Not only do we have to make Jesus Christ our Savior, but we must also make him our Lord.

When we have had the joy and privilege of helping someone come to know Jesus Christ as Savior, we cannot just leave it at that. Now we must explain to that person how important it is to have a daily walk with Christ, how crucial it is to make Him Lord, to give Him full sway and control in our lives.

I have never left a soul-winning experience without first explaining to the person that now that they have this new life, they need to water it and nurture it so that it can begin to take root and grow and blossom and give them strength on a daily basis. They need to cultivate a healthy prayer life and personal Bible study. That is the only way they will be able to overcome the fiery darts Satan will be throwing at them.

I try to help them realize that even though Satan no longer has their souls, he can still influence and wreak havoc in their lives. I try to explain to them that things will not get easier for them now. Quite the contrary, it may become even harder for them, because Satan will do all he can to make us miserable. The only way we can be victorious over his attacks is to allow the lordship of Jesus Christ to become preeminent within us. Jesus must become the Master of every area of our lives. Remember what we said about being joint heirs with Jesus Christ. Everything that belongs to Him now belongs to us. The same strength available to Him while on earth is available to us so we can resist Satan and his minions.

The Lordship of Jesus Christ in our lives is absolutely essential in order for us to have a victorious Christian walk, and to enjoy the peace and comfort that only Jesus can give.

Now that we have come to the end of *this* road and are about to turn down another in our journey in evangelism, we can see that evangelism is more than just "telling" someone about Jesus. It does, indeed, encompass many different experiences and truths. The wheel of evangelism has many different spokes which hold it together, and like any wheel, if one spoke becomes damaged or missing, the wheel loses some of its strength. Each spoke has its purpose. Every wheel has a centralized, focal point called the hub, out of which extends all those spokes. In evangelism that hub is the Holy Spirit. The spokes extend to the outer rim which holds it all together, and that rim is Jesus Christ.

Every witnessing experience, every experience of salvation, every subsequent Christian life rolls along on this wheel of evangelism…as we will discover in the pages to follow.

CHAPTER 2

BEING A FRIEND

I once heard a preacher say at a church growth conference, "Our churches need to be more like the local bar down the street. If more of our churches would have a similar atmosphere to that of one you find in the neighborhood pub, church growth would sky rocket." What exactly did he mean by such an apparently wild and crazy statement?

Of course, we know he was not advocating a riotous, drunken, loud, and lewd way for the church people to conduct themselves. However, he was trying to point out that when one goes into a bar, there is an uncommonly friendly atmosphere that cannot be found in our everyday lives. With all the pressures placed upon us, and all the stress we have to deal with on a daily basis, and everyone—from our boss at work, to the salesman at the door, to the loan officer holding our mortgage note, even to our family—wanting a piece of our lives, the world around us hardly feels like a friendly place. It seems like we can't be ourselves. We can't let our hair down. We can't laugh. We can't relax. But when one steps into a typical drinking establishment, everything changes. No one cares what walk of life you come from. They accept you for whom and what you are. Here is a place where you can relax and be yourself because you know others around you are just like you. Everyone can relate to and identify with each other, because all of you are experiencing the same struggles and difficulties, the same pain and heartache, the same disappointment with life. It seems everyone is a friend. You don't even have to know the other person's name, and even if it is just for the evening, you are able to strike up a friendship, because you realize that other person identifies with you. He's been there too.

If more churches would convey that kind of similar friendly atmosphere, perhaps more people would be in attendance in churches all across our country.

When it comes to witnessing to those who are lost without Christ, I have come to believe that these people actually need a friend more than a "preacher." Based upon the definition of evangelism we looked at in the previous chapter, I have reached the conclusion that evangelism may be more concerned with *"being"* than with *"doing"* and *"telling."* In this day in which we live I truly believe that *"friendship"* evangelism has become just as important as, and perhaps even more effective, than what may be referred to as *"confrontational"* evangelism.

I remember a pastor once sharing with me how embarrassed he was when he had taken a visiting revival speaker into the home of an unsaved person. My pastor friend told me that the visit had turned into a very aggressive confrontation between the visiting evangelist and the unsaved husband of a faithful church member. As the two preachers were walking the husband through the plan of salvation, the revivalist got off the chair he was sitting in and began crawling on his knees over to the husband. He began pleading and begging, "Oh, my dear brother, you must be saved! You need to commit your life to Jesus NOW! You need to embrace him as your savior NOW, brother! You can't go on like this, brother! If you do, you'll spend an eternity in hell, brother! You need to get saved NOW!" Well, obviously, that husband, who was typically a mild-mannered sort of guy, took about as much of that as he could, and then finally asked the two preachers to leave and never come back.

At the time my friend was telling me this, it had been almost two years since that incident, and he had never even been able to get to first base with that husband again. As a matter of fact, whenever the pastor would make a visit to that home and the husband happened to be there, he would leave the room or even just leave the house and wouldn't come back until he knew the pastor was gone. And not only that, the friction became so intense in that household, that the wife stopped attending church as regularly as she used to.

Yes, granted, this incident is perhaps more the exception rather than the rule. But it seems to support the fact that if we "confront" people about their need for Christ instead of trying to be a friend to them, trying to identify with their struggles, and relate to their needs, then we may be fighting a losing battle. We need to approach our evangelistic efforts in a way that will cause others to accept Christ as their savior because they *want* to, not because they feel they have been forced into it. Yes, they need to feel guilty about their sin, but that does not mean we have to lay a guilt trip on them.

As important as one-on-one witnessing is, the time has come for us to be more of a friend in our witnessing rather than a "preacher." That's because people today are more likely to respond to friendship than direct confrontation. It's very likely they could be turned off by hard-nosed tactics.

As Christians, we need to be more willing to be a friend to someone and relate to that person's needs and identify with where that person is, than taking the person through a step-by-step soul-winning interview. People seem to be more susceptible to that type of approach.

Don't misunderstand what I am saying. This is not to say we are relieved of our obligation to witness. We are never to set aside Jesus' command to tell others about Him. But oftentimes, before we can be allowed to do that, others need to know we are their friend, and we accept them just as they are. That's what Jesus did. I believe that the best evangelism takes place in the context of trust and respect. Perhaps our greatest witness is our deepest relationship.

As was mentioned earlier, perhaps evangelism is more concerned with *"being"* than with *"doing"* and *"telling."* But, once again, don't misunderstand what is being said here. The person who says, "I just let my life do the witnessing," is insufferably self-righteous. *No one* is *that* good. Somewhere along the line you will have to say a word about Jesus. However, in the same light, the person who speaks the gospel with his lips and does not live it is in terribly bad shape. That person is a hypocrite.

Allow me to digress for a moment. At the beginning of our study, we mentioned that "evangelism" comes from the Greek word, "euangelion." The person who does the proclaiming is an evangelist, and that term comes from the Greek word, "euangelistis," which simply means a messenger of good news, not necessarily a "preacher." Evangelism is just telling others the good news. An evangelist is someone who does the telling. He does not have to be a preacher to be an evangelist. He does not have to have a lot of theological, seminary training. All a person needs is a message of good news.

In the latter part of the sixth chapter of 2 Kings, we read how Ben-Hadad, king of Aram, had laid siege to Samaria, and how there was a great famine in the city. In chapter 7, verses 3-16, we read how four beggars, who were lepers, decided to surrender to the king of Aram. They had realized that whichever way the dice fell, they would be no better off. If they stayed in Samaria, they would die of starvation. If they surrendered to the king of Aram, and he decided to kill them, it would be the same end result.

They left Samaria, and went over to the camp of the Aramean king, but when they arrived there, the camp was completely deserted. We read in verses 6-7 the reason for the empty camp. *"The Lord had caused the Arameans to hear the sound of chariots and horses and a great army, so that they said to one another, 'Look, the king of Israel has hired the Hittite and Egyptian kings to attack us!' So they got up and fled in the dusk and abandoned their tents and their horses and donkeys. They left the camp as it was and ran for their lives."*

The four beggars began looting the camp of its food and clothing and riches. Then they began to speak among themselves, *"We're not doing right. This is a day of good news and we are keeping it to ourselves. Let's go at once and report this to the royal palace"* (vs. 9). And that is just what they did. The scripture goes on to say that the people of the besieged city went and *"plundered the camp of the Arameans"* (vs. 16). The siege was over and the people were saved from starvation and death because four despised lepers shared with the people the good news of salvation from their hopeless situation.

Let me repeat what I said a moment ago. Based upon this passage of scripture, in evangelism, all we need is a message of good news. In other words, according to this text, as evangelists, we as beggars can tell other beggars about the Bread of Life in Jesus.

Remember the story in John, chapter 4, of Jesus speaking to the woman at the well? After showing the woman her need of the Messiah in her life, and after embracing Jesus as that Messiah, she ran into the city and proclaimed, "Come, see a man!" Then we read that many of the Samaritans believed on Jesus.

I truly believe that in these two biblical instances the main reason that people found salvation is because someone was a friend to those in need. The lepers were unselfish and friendly enough to share their good news with the starving people of a besieged city; and Jesus was a friend to a downcast woman who was scorned by her neighbors.

Yes, *doing* and *telling* evangelism is very important. But *being* is just as important, if not more so.

In the evangelistic experience, people want to know that we are for real. They want to know and believe that we are not plastic. I use that term, "plastic," because I heard it for the very first time in that context several years ago when a young man to whom I was trying to witness used that term concerning me.

This was a man in his mid twenties. I was fresh out of seminary ready to set the world on fire. I was asked to go visit this young man. I was warned, however, to be prepared for an encounter that may be a little out of the ordinary. For the sake of family privacy, we'll just call him "John."

I remember the first time I visited his home. When I was let into the house by his parents, and introduced to their son, John greeted me with, "So, YOU'RE the new kid on the block, huh?" Don't misunderstand—and I was told this ahead of time—John was always very cordial and courteous, very friendly. I was just advised to expect some ideas from him that would oftentimes come out of left field. I'll spare you all the details, only to mention that turned out to be a mild understatement to say the least. John did indeed turn out to be a "different" sort of person, but at the same time he became a good friend.

John had made a decision for Christ a few years before, but it was one of those instances where the family and the church people were not so sure it had been a genuine conversion experience. They felt that way because of his lifestyle. Jesus said in Matthew 7:20, *"By their fruit you will recognize them."* John certainly was not bearing much fruit.

By the time I had met John, he had become involved in some drug use, and he had been investigating demonism and the occult. It was starting to get out of control, and it eventually consumed almost his every waking moment. I visited John fairly regularly to try to help him turn his life around and embrace the full control of Christ in his life. There were other instances when his family would call and ask if I could come right over because he was in "one of those moods." It was not at all unusual for me to be called to their home, at times, in the wee hours of the morning to try to talk to John and calm him down.

John was slipping farther and farther away and deeper and deeper into unknown and dangerous territory. It all appeared completely hopeless. It had gotten to the point where he was starting to threaten his family with violence as well as threatening his own destruction.

We would spend hours just talking about anything and everything. I did more listening than talking, and just when I thought we were getting somewhere, something inside him would pull him back. Here was a young man who was extremely intelligent, very knowledgeable, and a good friend, who was slowly slipping away from me and the Lord. Oftentimes, I left our encounters weeping out of frustration and heartbreak for this young man with so much potential who was being slowly but surely dragged into his own personal hell. It was not unusual for me to question God and ask Him, "Why?" To this day I have never received an answer.

I would like to say that the story of John ended on a happy note, but, unfortunately, I can't. He had been on such a hard, downward spiral for so long that something inside of him just would not let go of him...or he wouldn't allow it to. Apparently, Satan had gotten his claws so deeply imbedded in John's life that John would not allow them to be released. John's life ended tragically in a violent suicide. I had since moved to a different church at that time, and when one of his family members called me to inform me of that tragedy, I just wept.

John had made a decision for Christ as his Savior. But looking back on the subsequent events in his life, was John truly a Christian? I honestly cannot give a definitive answer to that question. I thank God that I don't have to be the one to make that judgment call.

I share all of this with you because of what John told me a short while after my first visit with him, and something he reiterated over the months and years of our friendship. He said the reason he felt he could always talk with me and confide in me is because I wasn't "plastic." I wasn't phony. I was the real deal. Something he had not seen much of in other preachers and Christians. I talked to him straight. I pulled no punches. I expressed my feelings and opinions without hesitation or apology. I told him how I truly felt about him and some of the things he was involved in. But I never judged him. I accepted him for who and what he was. I embraced him as a friend. I could relate to some of the pain and disappointment he had felt in his short life. I was willing to cry with him and hurt with him and try to help him carry some of his burden.

People want us to be genuine and not plastic. They want us to accept them for who they are. They don't want us to point fingers at them and accuse. They want to know that somebody just simply cares. They want to know that somebody loves them just the way they are. I believe that people will accept us and give us their ear if they are convinced we are real and have paid a price for what we believe.

I remember reading about a young, divorced, single mother who attended college on her own. She went on to become a successful and happy mother, housewife, businesswoman, and author. Part of her journey led her to pursue graduate work in religion and aging.

As a young university student, she struggled with low self esteem and guilt from her divorce. There were nights of drinking, smoking pot, diet pills, and attempts to find the right man. She was a pretty confused young mother.

At the time there were two neighbors who lived in the same building with their three children. They were evangelical Christians who often invited her to dinner.

The troubled young mother said, "There was no finger-wagging, no scolding, no threats of hellfire and brimstone. They just lived their faith quietly and simply. And they loved me. I can't tell you how powerful an experience that was. Never before had I met Christians who loved as Christ loved—who hung out with those who desperately needed unconditional love in order to heal from their psychic wounds. Jesus hung out with prostitutes and tax collectors; they hung out with me. Those good people took an interest in me, mentored me, encouraged me, and believed in me until I could learn to believe in myself. My life has never been the same."

When Jesus called Peter and Andrew to follow Him in Matthew 4:19, He said, "Come, follow me, and I will make you fishers of men." Jesus was talking about net fishing. For the sake of our discussion here, when you think about it, fishing with hooks and lines and bait involves a violent removal of the fish from their surroundings and also employs deceit. Fishing with a net involves catching fish together within their normal context.

It is much more natural and effective to share the Good News out of a relationship of trust, based on friendship. It may take longer, but almost invariably it is better received, and its results are more lasting.

From time to time we all get opportunities to tell others about Christ. But we need to remember that people tend to listen to those they trust. That means we need to cultivate genuine friendships with people who don't know Christ.

We stated earlier that our greatest witness is our deepest relationship. It is absolutely essential that we be reminded of that truth, and yet it is commonly overlooked. For many, sharing one's faith is something they do quickly. There is no time for developing relationships. There is no attempt to identify with people.

In Luke 10:1-16 where Jesus sent out the seventy to witness in the surrounding areas. He gave them instructions that necessitated their identifying with others. He told them to stay in the homes of those among whom they worked. He told them to eat their food, which required more than just a casual association with people. They could not obey Jesus' instructions and remain apart and aloof.

In the area where they were to share the Good News, there were many Gentiles. Possibly some of those Gentiles even hosted some of the seventy. What would it have meant for a Jew to stay in the home of a Gentile? Would Jesus have expected them to eat the Gentiles' unkosher food?

At any rate, Jesus' assignment must have meant considerable adjustments for the seventy. But, by the same token, we need to remember what we mentioned early on in our study. Jesus was not asking them to do something He had not already done Himself.

John 1:14 tells us, *"The Word became flesh and made his dwelling among us."* Just think of the adjustments *that* required. What must it have meant for Jesus to leave the eternal courts of heaven and identify with us in that way? What did it mean for Him to take on human flesh, to take on our infirmities, to become weak, to suffer and *die*? What did it mean for Him to leave heaven and to take up residence in decadent human society?

Yet not only is that what happened, but His whole pattern of ministry showed that this is the only truly effective way of reaching people with the Good News.

But we must never think that just because it is *Good* News we are bringing to them, that people are automatically going to be all ears to our message. We have to earn a hearing. And that means we need to build relationships. To build relationships, we must associate and identify.

So, what exactly is involved in "being a friend" in evangelism? As we continue down this particular avenue in our journey, we will be approaching a few stoplights. But before the light turns green for us to move forward, we will need to stop and survey the intersection and be sure we have our bearings correct, so we won't make a wrong turn and venture off in the wrong direction.

CHAPTER 3

THE ROAD TO BECOMING A FRIEND

*A*s we travel down the road named Friendship Evangelism, we will come upon a few stoplights at various crossroads, and we must be sure we continue in the right direction without turning down one of those side roads which intersect the main thoroughfare and cause us to take a bad detour. Detours are necessary sometimes when the main road is being worked on because it needs improvement. But the road of evangelism as demonstrated by Jesus needs no improvement.

Stoplight number one. When talking to others about their need for Jesus Christ in their lives, the first thing we need to do is *accept* them just the way they are. Of course, that does not mean we condone their wrong actions or attitudes. But it does mean we respect them as persons. We respect their cultural differences, peculiarities, and any other unique areas of their lives.

Salvation has nothing to do with cultural uniformity. It does not have anything to do with one's manner of dress or one's speech patterns or vocabulary. Salvation has nothing to do with a person's racial or national background.

Salvation is dependent upon faith alone. It is dependent on committing one's life to Jesus as Lord.

Remember part of our definition of evangelism speaks to the lordship of Jesus Christ. Not only must new converts embrace Jesus as Savior, but also as Lord. Perhaps that was the main problem with John whom we discussed in the previous chapter. After having experienced the event of salvation in Christ, he never continued on in the process of making Him Lord of his life. I'm sure all of us can relate to what happens when we stop making Jesus Lord of every area of our lives. We know the feeling of joylessness, discontent, and misery that brings into our lives. Let's face it. When we put someone or something else on that throne in our lives, which should only be occupied by Jesus, we are headed down a long and unhappy road...a road which will lead us along some really dangerous, disastrous, and sometimes tragic detours. We may think this or that particular detour is the right way to go only to eventually discover the bridge is out, and there is no place else to go but back the way we came.

To be effective in our evangelism, we need to accept others just like they are, regardless of what walk of life they come from. Despite their cultural, racial, and national backgrounds, people need to be made aware that it really does not make any difference. When we accept them with all their scars and flaws, it will be easier for them to open themselves to the news we are bringing them. When they realize that we, too, struggle with sin and self-centeredness, and sometimes remove Jesus from that throne, they will more readily welcome what we have to say to them.

Yes, culture, tradition, and lifestyle can be—and often are—enriching things. They may even reflect biblical sensitivity to stewardship and modesty. But they are not the criteria for participation in the body of Christ.

I have often wondered how often we let our cultural hang-ups get in the way of accepting a brother or sister who has decided to cast their lot with Jesus. I am convinced that it happens far more frequently than it should; and I am further convinced that we, as Christians, have not really worked very hard at overcoming it.

Over and over we read in the gospels how merciful and compassionate Jesus was to those who approached Him, no matter what their status in life. I believe that in his gospel Luke reveals more of this element of Jesus' character than any of the other gospels. That's probably due to the fact that not only being the only Gentile to write any portion of God's Word, he was also a physician in touch with the weaknesses and infirmities of people. On numerous occasions in Luke we see Jesus caring about and struggling with the hurts of people. Luke provides us with a realistic portrait of the humanity of Jesus. We see a beautiful picture of the Son of God in human flesh who can identify with and relate to all the same difficulties in life that we have to face. We see in Jesus Someone who experienced all that we experience except our sin, as Hebrews 4:15 tells us: *"We have one who was tempted in every way, just as we are—yet was without sin."*

Jesus cares about our needs and our hurts. We can draw near to Him because He knows how we feel. Just as our need for identity is met in a relationship with Jesus, so is our need for acceptance. Time and again we see many different types of people draw close to Jesus because they had experienced His acceptance of them.

One of the first examples of this from Luke which immediately comes to my mind is the touching incident in chapter 7:36-39 when a "sinful" woman came and washed the feet of Jesus with her tears and dried His feet with her hair. When Simon, the Pharisee, who had invited Jesus to dine with him, saw this, he said to himself, *"If this man were a prophet, he would know who is touching him and what kind of woman she is—that she is a sinner."* Of course, Jesus knew what kind of woman she was. But here we have a religious leader who is supposed to be an example for others, judging another person simply because of what "kind" of woman she was. Jesus loved and embraced this woman as someone in need. What delight there is to know that He accepts us completely and loves us tenderly.

As Christians attempting to bring others to a saving knowledge of Jesus Christ, we need to demonstrate this same element of Jesus' character. We need to accept those we are trying to reach just as they are.

Stoplight number two. We need to *love* those we hope to reach. One reason crowds followed Jesus wherever He went was their awareness that He loved them.

Just as His acceptance of them was apparent when He risked scorn by associating with tax collectors, prostitutes, lepers, and the like, so, also,

His love for them was apparent in His refusal to turn His back on anyone who came to Him: the poor, the lame, the blind, the demon-possessed, whoever had a need. Effective evangelism needs to be built upon love.

We cannot win most people by scaring them with talk about impending judgment, or laying on guilt trips. We cannot win most people through reasoning, no matter how eloquent an advocate we may be unless they can see that behind the warnings and behind the arguments is our genuine love for them.

That's why we gave our hearts to Christ. Not because God sent us a tract or argument, or threats, but because He sent us His Son and His love. He allowed us to experience first hand the love He has for all mankind. He has shown us what real love is all about. There is a verse from one of the songs I always liked to sing, "Head Over Heels," which says, *"I thought I knew what love was all about, for I had known the love of friends and family. But when I met the One who saved me I found out that this love was love I never thought could be."*

Jesus' invitation to us to be Good News people is an invitation to love. It is not just an invitation to *talk* about love, but to *practice* it. God did not send us a tract from heaven describing His love. He sent us a living demonstration of it—He sent us His Son! I remember reading somewhere a long time ago that *"The greatest proof of God's love is the life that <u>needs</u> His love to explain it."*

People respond to love. There is, of course, no guarantee of how great the immediate response will be, but nearly always there will be some noticeable response, and in the end, love will prevail. Nothing is more powerful than a genuine attitude of love. We need to genuinely love those we hope to reach for Jesus.

In this day and age people are aware, perhaps more than at any other time, what is real and what is not. If we do not demonstrate a sincere and authentic love, others will know it. When we come to that intersection marked "love," we dare not turn to the left or right. We need to be sure we stay on that straight road in front of us. Even if the side road looks so close to being the real thing that no one could tell the difference, we dare not take that detour. Believe me, eventually others will know if we are for real or not—if we are "plastic." Jesus was the real deal and people knew it... and they will know it in us as well.

Stoplight number three. We also need to *care* for those we hope to reach. For some, caring for those who have a need is only a matter of duty.

But biblical caring is the overflow of a heart that really loves people. True love for our neighbor always translates into action. Caring *about* people is never enough. We need to care *for* them.

Showing care for others is sometimes difficult because we feel awkward about it. But it doesn't have to be difficult. Perhaps it boils down to just not being afraid to try. A pattern of caring is what we cultivate with God's help and is in response to His love towards *us*.

I remember hearing a fellow pastor warning against what he referred to as "care-less evangelism." He explained that while care-less evangelism may result in some real conversions, there may be many more that are turned against Christianity. By the same token, others may conclude that Christianity is no more than a shallow, meaningless gimmick. Still others may go through life with a false assurance of salvation, and go to hell with a decision card in their pocket. When we approach others with care-less evangelism, we are skating on thin ice, and we are placing them out on that proverbial limb, and eventually the tree becomes very shaky, and they can very possibly plummet to their doom.

Our best opportunities for Christian witness come as a result of relationships of trust that have been built up over a period of time. Most of the time people are not automatically going to give an ear to the message we want so badly to share with them. But as they come to know that we accept them, love them, sincerely care for them, and are anxious to demonstrate that love in tangible ways, they will begin to open up.

Dr. Howard Hendricks told of his conversion experience. He recalls, "Humanly speaking, I might never have been saved if someone hadn't 'said it with love' to me. I was nine years old, a little terror. I was out playing marbles one day when a man named Walt came along and invited me to Sunday school. There was nothing appealing to me about anything with 'school' in it, so he made me another proposition—one I liked better. 'Wanna play a game of marbles with me?'

"After he'd wiped me out in marbles, he inquired, 'Wanna learn how to play this game better?'

"By the time he'd taught me how to play marbles over the next few days, he'd built such a relationship with me that I'd have gone anywhere he suggested. Of the thirteen boys in that class...eleven ended up in vocational Christian work."

The apostle Paul would have liked Walt's approach to evangelism. In 1 Corinthians 9:22, Paul states, *"I have become all things to all men so that by all possible means I might save some."* Often when believers think of evangelism, they talk about what others need to know. But here Paul stressed what he himself needed to become. His strategy of evangelism involved identifying with unbelievers whenever possible instead of retreating from them because of differences. In many ways he cultivated a flexible spirit. Trying to relate redemptively one day to a Jew and the next day to a Gentile demanded such flexibility. Everywhere, Paul tried to reach both Jew and Gentile alike by whatever means necessary.

Paul did not partake in the sins of others to try to win an audience for the gospel, or even excuse their sins. Rather, he willingly set aside secondary issues so that the real issue became clear: their need for the gospel. Paul was truly a fisher of men who would do what he had to do in order to catch a few fish.

We need to genuinely care for those to whom we are witnessing. We need to become part of their lives. We need to get down in the dirt with them, to cry with them, to laugh with them, to hurt with them. We need to let them know someone really does care. When we come to the intersection of "caring" in evangelism, if we turn off onto the road of "care-less evangelism," we will be taking a tragic detour which could very easily cause someone to come to a sudden, crashing halt at the end of their own life's road.

As Christians, if we are serious about Jesus' Great Commission, we cannot be satisfied with letting just the church reach a lost world. Making disciples goes far beyond merely putting money in an offering plate. It means injecting ourselves into the anguish and brokenness of people's lives because we care, and because that is what salvation is all about: making people whole again, recycling the wasted lives of men and women who are in the same condition we were once in.

If there is to be any hope of reaching a lost and dying world for Christ, our Christ is going to have to be a first-hand Christ of experience, not a second-hand Christ of doctrine. We are going to have to move Christ from the cabooses of our lives to the engines of our lives. We need to start being friends to those in need. We need to be alert to opportunities God brings our way to show others we care. We have good news of hope and purpose and everlasting life. We need to be willing to pass it on to those who do not have that good news.

As we study the lives of the first Christians, we see that they not only talked about the Holy Spirit, they were empowered by Him. They not only talked about reconciliation, they were reconcilers themselves. They not only talked about Jesus, they followed Him daily. Without those things you may have evangelism, but you don't have the gospel. The Good News is that Jesus is alive, and that means we have something *personal* to share. The only true testimony for Christ is a testimony that comes from a personal relationship with Him.

Remember when we discussed being a witness? A witness is not somebody who merely repeats what somebody else has told him, or who has mastered the art of getting the message across. A witness is someone who has experienced what he's talking about. The love of Christ becomes known to others through Jesus, because it is a reality in that person's life. God became visible to man. We need to make God visible to people. They need to see God in our lives.

To refer back to Paul's statement in 1 Corinthians 9:22, we realize that his example is more important than ever in our multicultural world. Take a close look at your attitudes today. Are you allowing an unwritten code of behavior to be a barrier to sharing the gospel? Do you have expectations that unbelievers must meet before you reach out to them? It's a hard question, but one that is worth some serious thought and self-examination.

Perhaps all of us need to get down on our knees more often and play a few games of marbles.

Now that we have clearly seen what road we are to travel in our evangelistic efforts, we need to be aware that even though we are on the correct route, there will still be some unavoidable bumps along the way, and a few obstacles in our path. It will not always be a smooth road. But we must fully understand that we cannot let these deter us from our mission nor prevent us from reaching our destination. With God's help and guidance we can circumvent these barriers, forge ahead, and then let's just see if God in His omnipotence won't eventually open a door for us to give an answer for the hope that is within us.

CHAPTER 4

EVANGELISM'S BATTLE WITH GOODNESS

*G*rowing up as a child in Kansas City, Kansas, we lived on a street named Cambridge. It was at the top of a steep hill called Cambridge Hill, but all of us just referred to it as simply, "The Hill." Everyone in the immediate, surrounding area, when they heard the phrase, "The Hill," knew exactly what you were referring to.

As an adult when I would describe how steep that hill really was, people would have difficulty believing the truth of it. They would give the typical response that when we get older, we tend to embellish some of our childhood memories. Since so many years have elapsed, what appeared be so big in our childish eyes, actually is not as we remember it when we physically go back to that scene that played such a significant role in our lives. But let me assure you, my friends, that is certainly not the case in this instance.

When the hill was initially constructed, the road crew had literally laid it out with grooves in the pavement to give the tires of automobiles more traction to climb it, and even then sometimes a car would not make it if it did not have a fast enough head start. In the wintertime when snow was on the ground, there was absolutely no way at all for a vehicle to drive up that hill. I don't think even a bulldozer could have made it up that hill when it was packed with snow. The snow removal teams would not even attempt to clear "The Hill" of its snow. It was that steep. The back side of the hill dead ended at the front yard of a house. I'm sure you can imagine how much fun we neighborhood kids had riding our sleds down that hill when it was covered with snow.

In a reflective moment my sister and I sat down one day to try to figure out how many neighborhood kids lived on "The Hill" and within a one-block radius. We came up with around thirty different names, and all but about six of them lived up on "The Hill." That is rather amazing when you consider (as I found out much to my surprise several years ago when I made a nostalgic trip back there) that that one block on which we lived was really not all that long. Houses in close proximity of each other lined both sides of the street. Their front yards were not all that spacious, but most of the backyards were a fairly nice size for that type of community. It was very much a family-oriented neighborhood.

So, you may ask, what does all this have to do with our subject of evangelism?

My father was the pastor of an American Baptist church which sat on its own little grassy hill about a typical city block from Cambridge Hill. As a matter of fact, you could stand at the crest of "The Hill" and look out over the tree tops that dotted the open field in front of you and see the church's pearly white structure in the distance. Several of the families and most of the children on our block attended the church.

There was a dear, sweet, little old lady who lived two houses down from us with her husband. Janice was one of the sweetest, godliest, warmest Christians you could ever know. She never missed a Sunday in church. Not only was she a wonderful Christian, but she was just an all around good-hearted person. She would do absolutely anything for you. I can't even imagine how many delicious dishes and desserts she would carry over to her preacher and his family.

Her husband, on the other hand, was an entirely different story. Every neighborhood has one. Ours was no different. He was the "grumpy old man," "the grouch," "the old coot" on the block. To this day I still don't know what his first name was. I suppose it's because, unfortunately, I never took the time to find out. All of us kids just referred to him as "Old man, Stevens." My sister and I were discussing this very thing in my preparation for writing this chapter and neither one of us could actually say we had ever known his first name, and I think that is rather sad. I look back on that time with regret and chagrine because I really don't think any of us ever gave him a chance.

I have come to believe that we were unfair to Mr. Stevens, because in my childlike manner I saw a side of him that probably none of the other children saw. Because of that, I did not harbor the same severe opinion of him that my friends did, although my opinion still was not as it should have been. Like all children we prejudged "different" people unkindly.

We had a little dog named Aristotle. What Aristotle loved to do more than anything else was spend hours outside playing with a Folgers coffee can. It *had* to be Folgers. Trust me. You could not fool him with a different brand name even it was in a red can. He would stick his nose down inside the can, yelp twice into the can, and on the third yelp he would toss that can back over the top of his head and then chase after it.

Back then a pound of coffee was bought in a squat little can, which after it was opened, had a metal rim around the top of the can. As Aristotle would play with the can the rim would eventually come off leaving a razor-sharp edge. After a while of playing with the can in that condition, the edge would cut into Aristotle's nose, causing it to bleed.

Mr. Stevens would sit in his back yard two houses down and watch that dog play and play and play. He thought it was the cutest thing.

One day while Mr. Stevens was walking down the alley behind our backyard, he noticed Aristotle's nose was bleeding. Being the observant person he was, he immediately summed up the situation. Unbeknownst to any of us, he unlatched the gate, walked into the yard, and picked up the coffee can and took it over to his little shed in his own backyard. Being the friendly dog he was (unless there was an obvious threat), Aristotle let him do so.

A few minutes later he came back over and knocked on our back door. Mom answered the door and he asked, "Is Gene here?" Mom invited him inside, but he declined. He stood on the back porch waiting for me to come out of my bedroom. When I came out on the porch that "old coot" on the block stooped down to the level of a ten year old boy, held out that coffee can and showed me what he had done, and explained how I could do the same thing. He said if I had any trouble with it, I could come over anytime to ask him to help me, which is exactly what I did the first time.

That crusty old man, whom all the kids on the block thought did not have a soft spot anywhere in him, had taken the time to use his hammer to pound down the razor edge of the coffee can and then pound the lip flat against the inside of the can, making it as dull as a table knife. He smiled at me (actually smiled!) and said, "Gene, this way little Aristotle can play as long as he wants with his coffee can and never hurt himself again."

I cannot say we became close friends after that, but I do remember seeing him in an entirely different light. Unlike Dorothy's tin man, he actually had a heart.

Mr. Stevens had a vacant lot just on the other side of the alley which ran behind our house. It was about fifty feet long and thirty feet wide, and it was a perfect place for the neighborhood kids to gather to play. But when Mr. Stevens saw the kids out there playing, he would run outside yelling at them to get off his property, using a few choice words. But when "his" preacher's son was with them, he didn't care at all. Not only that, but whenever "his" preacher's son wanted to play out there, he could do so as long as he wanted. I always thought that was interesting about him. In the six years Dad pastored that church, never once did Mr. Stevens ever darken its doors; and yet I was "his" preacher's son.

I have shared all of this history with you for a reason, and despite how it appears, it *is* all relevant to our discussion.

After I had become a pastor myself, Dad and I were sitting in his living room one afternoon discussing evangelism and reaching people for Christ. I don't remember how or why I even brought up the subject, but I asked him, "Dad, do you remember Mr. Stevens who lived a couple of houses down from us up on "The Hill?"

He replied, "Oh, sure. I remember him."

I said, "Well, you used to visit him and his wife frequently. Tell me about him. From what I remember, she was one of the sweetest persons anyone would ever want to know. But he was a really crotchety old man who never seemed to have time for church or anything to do with church. He was a real piece of work, that guy was. How his wife managed to live with him I'll never know. She was a real saint indeed. She must have an extra star in her crown because of it. Now that he's in eternity, I wonder what he thinks of church now."

In that gentle, fatherly, gracious, and Christlike way of his that my sister and I knew all too well, he said, "Now, now, son. You don't know what eternity held in store for him. That is not for us to judge. We never know the whole story about things like this."

I looked at him and said, "Yeah, I know, Dad. But…come on, now."

He said, "Well, let me tell you something about 'old man Stevens' as you kids called him. Well…what little I know, that is. I don't think anyone, even his wife, ever knew the whole story." Then in that wise manner of his he began to shed some light on this rather mysterious person who never had much to say to anybody, and who came across as one of the unfriendliest men you would ever know.

Mr. Stevens and Janice had been married for a good number of years, and one would think that if anyone knew what made a person tick, it would be the spouse with whom he had lived most of his life. But when asked, Janice would simply say that she did not know the cause of her husband's deep bitterness and dislike of the church or anything church- related. For a long time she tried to get him to open up, but he never would. He would not so much as shed even a glimmer of light upon why he had such deep-seated feelings. When she realized he would never talk about it, and would even become seriously agitated if pushed too far, she finally gave up trying.

All that his wife knew—and that from family members—was that before they were married, he had attended church very faithfully. But something very serious happened in his life that had to do with church, and he became totally turned off by the very thought of church and Christianity. He completely refused to ever discuss it with anyone. No one really knows what it was, but it left such a deep, lasting scar on his life that nothing could ever remove it.

Dad told me he tried many times to get Mr. Stevens to talk about it, using every rational and psychological argument he could think of as to why it would be good for him to let it all out. But nothing worked. When Dad would try to talk to him about the love of Christ, he would tell Dad that he just did not want to hear it nor discuss it. Dad said, "And that was that. I could never, *ever* get one foot off home plate, let alone get to first base with him."

Dad went on to explain, "But by the same token, son, he was a decent man. He really did have a good heart…for the most part. He loved his wife immensely and was totally devoted to her, and there was nothing that he would not do for her." Dad went on to say, "I know that doesn't fit the picture that everyone had of him, but as strange as it sounds, that is the truth."

I asked Dad what he thought of Mr. Stevens' spiritual condition because the Bible does teach us about eternal security. Since he had attended church so regularly at one time and was active, did he think that possibly Mr. Stevens was one of those Christians who would have very little or no reward in heaven, yet *"saved, but only as one escaping through the flames"* as Paul states in 1 Corinthians 3:15.

Dad answered, "I guess we'll never know till we get there ourselves. I'm glad I don't have to make that decision, that we have a far wiser, more competent Judge to do that."

In evangelism, when we come face to face with "goodness" in an individual, we are probably confronting the toughest obstacle we will ever meet. When we talk about a good and loving God, we are engaging in what has always been one of the most controversial topics of discussion concerning salvation, and sometimes even with the help and power of God's Holy Spirit, we can never overcome that obstacle. We have all heard it said more than once: *"I cannot believe that a loving God..."*

I'm sure we all agree that there really are some good, decent people in our world. The kind of people who would do anything in the world for you. Good-hearted, loving, considerate, people who would literally give you the shirt off their backs or the last dollar in their pockets. The kind who would, at a moment's notice, drop what they are doing and come to help someone in need, no matter what the cost. The kind who would make any sacrifice to lend a hand, expecting nothing in return. Quite the contrary, they may even be offended or insulted at the very thought that you would want to repay them for their act of kindness. The type of person who would never do any harm to anyone or anything. These people may even go to church and be faithfully involved in all its activities. And almost anyone who knows these people would say without hestiation, "If anyone deserves to go to heaven, they do. Surely, God can see that."

Despite how admirable all these characteristics are in a person, the Bible is very explicit in its declaration concerning the "lostness" of human beings, and very clear in its instructions on how to overcome that hopeless condition that plagues every single person, no matter how "good" he or she is.

Romans 3:23 tells us *"All have sinned and fall short of the glory of God."* God makes no exceptions here. He does not say "All have sinned and fall short except those who are good-hearted, decent people." God tells us He is no respecter of persons (Romans 2:11).

Without Christ in our lives we are all the same. We are all hopelessly driving down a road that ends in despair and eternal separation from God. If all the "goodness" in the world could somehow be channeled into our lives, it would still not be enough to warrant our acceptance before a holy and righteous God. In Romans 3:10 and 12, the apostle Paul writes, *"There is no one righteous, not even one…there is no one who does good, not even one."*

"Goodness" is one of the biggest bumps in the road of evangelism. Some people may have the idea that, "I'm just as good as that person," and no doubt they very likely could be. They may be even better; and the sad part about it is that the actions and lifestyles of a lot of "good" people could possibly be better than that of some Christians. We've all heard it said more than once, "If that's what Christianity is all about, no thank you. I think I'll just pass." How tragic is that?

Despite the fact that these "good" people may appear to have a more admirable lifestyle than some "worldly" Christians, nevertheless there is one defining factor which separates this kind of Christian from the unsaved, "good" person: they have Christ in their lives. Paul refers to these kinds of

Christians as "carnal" (KJV) in 1 Corinthians 3:1. No, these Christians may not receive any rewards in heaven, but they will make it through those pearly gates. Don't misunderstand. I am not advocating that once we become a Christian, we can live any way we please. That was the whole problem Paul was addressing in his first letter to the Corinthians. That kind of a Christian lifestyle is a travesty, a tragic waste of all the benefits God offers us in His Son, Jesus. Those who live such a life miss out on so much joy and love and peace unnecessarily.

But getting back to this idea of "goodness," a person can read the Bible everyday, go to church faithfully, sing in the choir, attend Bible study, tithe regularly, and treat his fellow

human beings with the greatest amount of consideration and caring, and still not be good enough to enter God's Kingdom. Even with all of those qualities going for us, we are still damaged goods.

A primary example of this can be seen in the familiar incident of the rich young ruler as found in Matthew 19:16-22. The young man approaches Jesus and asks, *"What good thing must I do to get eternal life?"* We see here where this young man places his emphasis in the question he asks. "What *good* thing must I do?"

Jesus responded to the young man's question by instructing him to obey the commandments. The young ruler asked in return which ones did Jesus mean? Jesus singled out murder, adultery, stealing, lying, respecting his parents, and treating others as he would want to be treated.

The young man replies, *"All these I have kept. What do I still lack"* (vs. 20). In Mark's and Luke's writing of this same incident the young man answers Jesus by saying, *"All these I have kept since I was a boy,"* implying that virtually all his life this young man had been a really decent, good kind of person, always treating his family and others with respect and consideration; and no doubt he probably did.

Now Jesus, knowing this man's heart, mentioned only these last six of the Ten Commandments for a reason. He was addressing this man's horizontal relationship with his fellow human beings. Jesus purposely did not refer to the first four of the Ten Commandments which speak to one's vertical relationship with God, because in His wisdom Jesus knew what was missing in this rich young ruler's life.

When the young man asked, *"What do I still lack?"*, going straight to the heart of this young man's problem, Jesus told him to sell everything he had, give the proceeds to the poor, then he will have treasures in heaven, and be unencumbered enough to follow Jesus. We read that *"When the young man heard this, he went away sad, because he had great wealth"* (vs. 22).

What a tragedy this is. Yet, it is a story that is repeated in the lives of so many individuals all across our society. Regardless of how "good" we may be, regardless of how wonderfully we treat our family and our fellow human beings, if there is any area in our lives that we refuse to turn loose of so that God, through His Son, can have the preeminence in our lives, we cannot be fit for the Kingdom of God. Like this young man, it could be our wealth or some other material things in our lives. It could be our job, our home, our family. It could be anything we place before God that prevents us from surrendering our hearts and lives and wills completely over to Him. As long as we are encumbered by these things to the point we are not willing to give them up for Jesus, we cannot be accepted by Him. But by the same token, for clarification, I feel we need to point out a very significant truth regarding this issue.

This command of Jesus—this expectation from God—can be disheartenting and misunderstood by a lot of people. In my years of Bible study I have come to believe that God is not literally telling us we actually have to give up all these things in our lives to follow Him. My understanding is that

God just wants us to be *willing* to give them up, if it were to come to that. Naturally, He wants us to give up our sinful lifestyle. But when it comes to the comforts and joys He has made possible for us, He is not really asking us to turn our backs on those. He's only asking us to be *willing* to do so. He's asking us, "Do you love me enough, do you trust me enough to do anything I ask of you no matter what?" He asked Abraham the very same question: "Do you love me enough, Abraham, to give up the dearest and most precious thing in your life for me?" God did not really want to take Isaac from Abraham. All he wanted was Abraham's willingness to do as he was asked.

That is the test each of us must face if we are sincere in wanting to follow Jesus. That is the test that so many "good" people fail. Jesus told us we cannot come to God through our goodness. He told us in John 14:6, *"No one comes to the Father except through me."*

In evangelism, when we come face to face with "goodness" it could very likely be the toughest battle we have to fight.

I remember in one of my previous churches how delighted I was to see an older couple walk through the church doors one Sunday morning. They had lived in the area of a previous church where I had served. When I walked over and hugged both of them I asked what brought them to my neck of the woods. They said they had just moved into the general area and wanted to come visit us. They were dear, dear friends and I had had the joy of visiting in their home a number of times and having dinner with them, and the privilege of returning that favor more than once.

She had to be one of the sweetest, godliest Christian women I ever had the pleasure of knowing. Although he had not attended church very regularly with her previously, once they moved into our area, her husband (we'll call him Ralph) began coming to church with her quite faithfully, and attending a lot of the church functions.

Ralph was one of the most intelligent and knowledgeable men I had ever known. He just seemed to know so much about almost anything. We had so many enjoyable, interesting conversations about almost every subject one could think of. I always appreciated his feedback concerning certain ideas, and I was amazed at his insight into so many subjects. I could sit and talk with him and listen to him for hours and never get tired of it. He was just a good, good, decent, upstanding gentleman who was devoted to his wife, always seemed to have a kind word for someone, and always tried to see the good in everyone. He was indeed a very good friend.

However, by his own admission Ralph was not a Christian. But that did not prevent us from having lengthy, in-depth discussions about the Bible, God, Jesus, and Christianity in general. He was never unwilling to talk about the one subject that was always uppermost in my mind when we would visit. Our conversations never got out of control, were never heated, and we were never condescending nor insulting to each other's opinions.

As I had seen in others before, his intellectual, logical approach to life hindered his embracing Christianity's concept of a real God and salvation by grace alone. He had once acknowledged to me that he supposed he was a self-proclaimed agnostic, someone who denied God's existence is provable, somebody who believes that it is impossible to know whether or not God exists. He believed there must be some kind of "supreme being" or "supreme something" out there who is responsible for all we see around us; but is it God? We'll just never know.

No matter how many different ways I tried to explain it, he just could not wrap his head around this idea of complete faith without seeing proof with one's own eyes. He told me one evening after having dinner with them, "Gene, you know me well enough to know that I don't mean any offense to you when I say what I'm going to say. But as convincing as your arguments and reasoning sounds, I guess I will never know in this life if all that you say is true. And if there is indeed an afterlife, I guess I'll know then. But right now I just can't rationally accept what you are saying." We continued to have several similar discussions after that, but I never could get any farther with him than before.

I cannot even begin to count the number of hours I prayed for Ralph's eternal soul, how much I begged for God's guidance to just say the right thing at the right time that would turn Ralph's mind around. But in God's omniscient wisdom for whatever reasons He may have had, it was not meant to be.

More than once Ralph had said to me if God is as loving and just and fair as I proclaimed, he felt sure when it came his time to go, and there was a place we all went to after this life, then God would certainly take into consideration the kind of man Ralph was. My heart would just ache when I would hear him make such statements. He would say that if what the Bible says is true about goodness versus the grace of God, then, of course, it made sense what I was saying. But, there again, it came back to that faith issue, and that was something he was not prepared to accept.

Later, after I moved away from the area, I eventually lost touch with Ralph and his wife. Did something ever click in his mind or heart that finally made him see the realization of his own hopeless condition and accept the truth of God's Word? When he stepped out of this life and into a life of eternity, did he step into the light of heaven and the presence of Jesus, or the darkness of an eternal separation from God? I don't have an answer to such questions. I wish I did. To reiterate what he said: I guess I'll know when I get there.

Perhaps you are wondering why we have spent so much time—an entire chapter on this subject, dwelling on this unpleasant bump in the road. This is a book about evangelism, soul winning, reaching others for Christ, telling the joyful Good News of salvation in Jesus. Why this "morbid" and rather depressing departure into an area which seems so disheartening and discouraging? Well, my friend, that *is* the reason.

So often we hear about and talk about the joys of evangelism, the look of happiness and peace we see on the faces of newly converted individuals, the uplifting feeling of seeing the lives of persons transformed by the love of Jesus, the ecstasy we experience knowing that the long-awaited answer to prayer has finally come. But there is another side of evangelism I feel is too often neglected, a side which can bring disappointment, a sense of failure, a feeling of defeat.

Did you ever stop to realize that the Bible is a military book? From Genesis to Revelation, we read such words as war, battle, fighting, armor, soldier, conquest, weapons. We have to understand as evangelists, we are engaged in warfare. We are constantly fighting. The apostle Paul writes in Ephesians 6:12, *"For our struggle is not against flesh and blood, but against the rulers, against the authorities, against the powers of this dark world and against the spiritual forces of evil in the heavenly realms."*

We are at war, and Satan will do anything and everything to try to prevent us from winning that war. Whatever excuses, whatever reasonings, whatever arguments, whatever self assurances of the overall goodness of man he can place in the hearts and minds of lost individuals to keep them from embracing our message of Good News, he will do so. And in doing so, he can also cause us to become disillusioned and disheartened. If we let him, Satan can bring about within us a defeatist attitude, and a feeling of failure and lack of accomplishment.

Yet we have to remember, that in *any* war, not every battle that is fought will end in victory. Some battles will be lost. Spiritual warfare is no different. When we face Satan and his army, we need to remember that he is a strong and persuasive general. Like many deluded dictators in history who were able to persuade their soldiers to go to their deaths believing in their general's lost cause, the devil's followers will go to their graves believing with all their hearts that they are in the right. As Christians, we dare not let this distract us from our goal. We dare not let this deter us from our mission. We dare not allow this to take our eyes off the prize of the high calling of Christ.

Paul writes to Timothy in 2 Timothy 2:1 and 3: *"Be strong in the grace that is in Christ Jesus...endure hardship like a good soldier of Christ Jesus."* Paul goes on to say in verse four that a soldier wants to please his commanding officer.

As Christian soldiers, we want to please our Commander in Chief. We need to be strong in the grace that is in Christ Jesus. We cannot be strong, we cannot please our Commander if we are allowing Satan to cause us to be discouraged, disillusioned, and ready to give up the fight. We need to be faithful to our mission and to Christ's Great Commission. We are shut up to a glorious cause. Let's allow the glory of Christ and His love to shine forth from us despite the fact that we see some walk away from the message we bring them. Let's allow others to see our untiring, ceaseless efforts to win them to a saving knowledge of Jesus, to show them that we accept them, care for them, and love them.

The apostle Paul writes in 1 Corinthians 15:57, *"Thanks be to God! He gives us the victory through our Lord Jesus Christ."* And because of that he goes on to say, *"Therefore, stand firm. Let nothing move you. Always give yourself fully to the work of the Lord, because you know that your labor in the Lord is not in vain"* (vs. 58). We must never give up the fight. We *will* eventually be victorious. Yes, a few battles may be lost, but the war will ultimately be won. We have a glorious promise from God in Galatians 6:9: *"Let us not become weary in doing good, for at the proper time we will reap a harvest if we do not give up."* What greater promise could God give us in evangelism? Be strong. Be diligent. Be encouraged because *God* is on our side. And if God be for us, who can be against us…and win?

Yes, on the road of evangelism we will come across a few bumps and face a few obstacles, and the "goodness" of man is just one of them. But no matter how rough the bump, no matter how insurmountable the obstacle appears, the road will eventually become smooth again, and the obstacles will eventually disappear as long as we let Jesus do the driving, and let God's Holy Spirit be the power behind us that keeps us moving forward to our destination at the end of the road.

CHAPTER 5

APATHY: A MAJOR BUMP IN THE ROAD

*A*t the risk of sounding redundant by repeating what we discussed in chapter three regarding Stoplight Number Three concerning caring, I feel it is necessary to address this major bump in our road of evangelism. There are two sides to this bump called "apathy," both of which can be harmful to the ones we are trying to evangelize, and also to ourselves.

When apathy positions itself into the hearts of people, it can cause some serious damage. When people just don't care, it is extremely difficult to overcome this obstacle, to smooth out this bump in their lives. Nothing we say or do seems to get through to them. They simply don't care.

It reminds me of a classroom incident I read about several years ago. A teacher asked her class of lackadaisical, half-hearted students, "What is apathy?" No one responded. She asked again, "Come on now. What do you think it means?" Finally, a slouching student in the back raised his hand. The teacher asked for his answer. He just shrugged his shoulders, waved his hand in a way of dismissing the question as unimportant and just simply drawled, "Who cares?"

On the surface that student's answer could possibly come across as a little humorous, and I guess it is when you think about it. But, unfortunately, that is the attitude of far too many people, and it is sending a lot of those persons off into an eternity of separation from God.

If we let it, there are at least two ways that I see where apathy can cause us to stumble in our evangelistic efforts, and prevent us from fulfilling Jesus' Great Commission. As with any bump, there are two sides—a top side and a bottom side—that, although similar, differ in how it seeks to block, or at the least, slow down evangelism.

Side number one. The top side of this bump called "apathy" is, by its very nature of being on top, the most obvious.

There are more people than not who don't care about the message we bring to them. They're not at all interested. They would just as soon go on with their lives as they are, rather than consider such heavy issues as dying and spending an eternity in heaven or hell. Because of that, they refuse to hear anything which would involve changing their lifestyle—which would involve "turning over a new leaf." Of course, if you were to ask them, they would say, naturally, they want to go to heaven when they die, if there is such a place.

That reminds me of the song country artist, Kenny Chesney, made popular in which he sings, *"Everybody wants to go to heaven, but nobody wants to go now."* Certainly, they want to hear the good Lord call their names when they stand outside those pearly gates, but they would rather He waited a number of years before that happens. They're having too much fun down here...or they have too much they feel they still have to do.

Don't misunderstand. I am not eager to die anymore than the next person. However, I do have a feeling of peace within me that when that day does come, I need not worry about the outcome. That is part of the Good News that we have to try to impress upon those to whom we are witnessing.

Two incidents in the Bible immediately come to mind when I think about this bump, apathy.

First, in Matthew 24:38-39, Jesus refers to the time of Noah and the great flood. He says, *"For in the days before the flood, people were eating and drinking, marrying and giving in marriage, up to the day Noah entered the ark; and they knew nothing about what would happen until the flood came and took them all away."*

Regardless of the years and years of preaching to scores of individuals, they just ignored the warnings of Noah. They laughed and scoffed at him. They went about their everyday lives not caring and not believing what would happen. Their doom was universal. Neither rich nor poor escaped. The literate and the illiterate, the admired and the abhorred, the religious and the profane, the old and the young, all sank in one common ruin.

Those who ridiculed Noah, those who judged him as being insane, even those who may have spoken patronizingly of this old man's faithfulness to his convictions, but did not share them, were all drowned in the same sea. The flood swept them *all* away and did not make a single exception. Even so, outside of Christ, final destruction is certain for every person. No rank, possession, or character will be sufficient to save a single soul who has not believed in the Lord Jesus. How foolish. There was not one wise man left upon the earth outside of the ark. None of them cared. How destructive is apathy!

Secondly, I see in the book of Nahum a perfect example of how the apathy of a people can bring about serious and inevitable destruction.

We know that Jonah had been sent to the great city of Nineveh to preach about the salvation that God wanted to bring to them to avoid their imminent destruction. Despite being such a reluctant, hard-hearted prophet, God was still able to use someone even like Jonah to successfully get His message across to a wicked nation. As a result of that we see that an entire city with as many as six hundred thousand people *"turned from their evil ways"* (Jonah 3:10), and a great, miraculous revival broke out everywhere in Nineveh. I have often said that the *greatest* miracle of the book of Jonah, is that God could *use* Jonah at *all*. But, unfortunately, what some biblical scholars have referred to as "the greatest revival in the history of the world," was rather short-lived. It lasted less than a hundred years. Enter the prophet, Nahum.

Like Jonah, Nahum came preaching imminent doom for this wicked, sinful city. The Ninevites had fallen back into their previous lifestyles. In the book of Nahum we see the death of a city. Strange as it may sound, the city had sinned itself to death. But the tragedy is that it was living so well after Jonah had preached God's warning to them a hundred years earlier. A sermon that only took eight words to proclaim: *"Forty more days and Nineveh will be overturned"* (Jonah 3:4). That is probably the shortest sermon ever preached and yet look at what the results were.

But one hundred years later, the city of Nineveh had for all intents and purposes died. Spiritually, it was doomed. Its fall was imminent and certain. When Nahum brought his message of judgment, the city did not even kick or scream. It did not resist or repent. It did not attempt to argue with God or His spokesman. It just rolled over and died. And there's a reason for that, which we will address when we look underneath at the bottom side of this bump in the road.

Not heeding the warnings of Nahum, the Ninevites did nothing to prepare themselves for the approaching enemy. Their guards on the watchtowers did not remain alert. The king and city officials failed to warn their citizens that danger was nipping at their heels. The military generals and strategists refused to reinforce the city's walls and fortifications. No one cared. They all felt they had nothing to worry about. After all, Nineveh was probably one of the strongest fortified cities of the ancient world. The Ninevites felt forever secure behind their one-hundred-foot walls…walls so thick that some believe they were wide enough for six chariots to ride abreast of each other on top of them.

Yet, just as God had warned through His prophet, those walls came down and that great city was laid waste when the Babylonian army came marching mercilessly in conquest. So complete and effective was the judgment of God on Nineveh that the existence of the city disappeared for ages.

We need to take God seriously. Nineveh did not do that. At one time Nineveh's citizens listened to God speak through Jonah and responded in repentance and reverence. But time passed, and the people forgot. They reverted to their evil, vicious patterns of living and got back to business as usual, without one solitary thought about the God who is King above all other gods. And they would pay the ultimate price. God's patience would run out, and destruction would come.

Nahum, like all the other prophets in their own way and in their own time proclaimed one serious message loud and clear: Don't mess around with God! Because they did not care, the Ninevites realized how serious that message really was.

Before we flip this bump over to examine the bottom side, there is one other incident in the ministry of Jesus I feel warrants our close study, which reveals another aspect of apathy. It's found in Luke 12:13-20 where we read the Master's parable of the rich fool.

We are all familiar with the story. A rich man's ground produced a bountiful harvest. As a result of this, he ran out of barns in which to store all his crops. He was in a quandary. What could he do? We read he said to himself, *"This is what I'll do. I will tear down my barns and build bigger ones, and there I will store all my grain and goods. And I'll say to myself, 'You have plenty of good things laid up for many years. Take life easy; eat, drink, and be merry'"* (vss. 18-19). This man was going to sit back and enjoy his wealth and prosperity because, no doubt being in good health, he had all the time in the world to enjoy life. So, why should he worry or care about such nonessential issues like the condition of his eternal soul? Yet God had other plans for this man. We read in verse 20, *"But God said to him, 'You fool! This very night your life will be demanded from you.'"*

Too many people are dropping off into an eternity of darkness because they feel they have all the time in the world to make a decision for Christ. I have always felt this is probably one of the most devious and diabolical schemes that Satan has ever devised to prevent individuals from embracing Jesus as their Savior. Perhaps he does not try to brainwash them with the excuse that there is no God or that the Bible is not true or even that Jesus is not "the way, the truth, and the life," so much as he convinces them that, "Yes, if you do believe Jesus is your only road to salvation, then that's fine, but there's no need to make such a drastic decision right now. You have a lot of time yet. Just wait a while. Maybe next time."

I remember my father in the ministry, Dr. Bob, once telling me about an incident when he and an associate evangelist were holding a week's revival in a town in Arkansas. At the end of the week, there had been very little response to their preaching and teaching. The residents of the town just did not seem to care much at all for the Good News being proclaimed. As they were leaving town on Sunday evening at the conclusion of the meeting and had reached the city limits, Dr. Bob's friend said, "Bobby, stop the car." When Dr. Bob had pulled the car to the side of the road, his friend stepped out, looked back at the city they were leaving, and stomped his feet. When he got back inside the car, Dr. Bob just looked at him questioningly. His friend quoted Luke 9:5 to him: *"Whosoever will not receive you, when ye go out of that city, shake off the very dust from your feet for a testimony against them"*(KJV).

Dr. Bob told me that when he heard his friend say that, an eerie feeling came over him. He went on to say that one month later a tornado came through and virtually leveled that

town, killing a number of people and leaving a lot of families without homes and wiping out a great many important businesses, essentially bankrupting a lot of the owners. He said it took a good part of a year before that town ever recovered from the devastation.

Several years ago I was leading one of several evangelistic teams who were holding crusades in South Korea sponsored by the Southern Baptist Convention. Two days before we were scheduled to return to the states, I was in the home of a family along with my two team members and our interpreter. We had been witnessing to the unsaved husband of one of the members of the church where we had been conducting our crusade.

He was a rather belligerent man who kept arguing against us and our message. He was saying he really did not care to hear such nonsense. What we were sharing with him was ridiculous, and no one could know what lies on the other side of death. When we died we were all like the animals which just lay in the ground rotting away. After he'd had enough of our talk, he told us to get out and take our Jesus with us. He didn't care about Him and had no need of Him in his life.

Two days later on the morning we were to fly out, I received a call at my hotel from the pastor of that church. He told me that during the previous night this same man, who was in excellent health, was working out in his yard and suddenly dropped over dead from a serious heart attack.

Could these two incidents be examples of God's judgment on people who, in their apathy and indifference, refused to accept the Good News of Jesus Christ which was brought to them? I have no way of knowing, and I am not even going to try to speculate on such possibilities. That is not my place to do so. However, I do know, as was the case with Nineveh, God means business; and when God does His work, it is thorough and conclusive. And the judgment is always severe!

Side number two. We have spent a great deal of time discussing the apathy in individuals which confronts us when we are trying to witness to them. But the underneath side of this bump in the road can, at times, be just as detrimental. I am talking about the apathy which can exist within our own lives.

For the most part, I do not believe that we, as Christians, develop this harmful trait mainly because we just do not care for the souls of others. I truly believe that most of us are genuinely concerned about the lost condition of those without Christ. After all, if we sincerely love the Lord and are appreciative of all that He has done for us, why would we not desire for others to experience this same peace and joy that we have?

No, I don't believe it is because we do not want other individuals to know Christ as their Savior and do not care if they do. But perhaps the problem is that we do not care all that much to *do* the witnessing ourselves. It could be that the attitude of far too many Christians is, "Let somebody else do it."

There are pastors and evangelists (in the professional sense of the word) who can express to others this Good News. There are chaplains in hospitals, in nursing homes, in prisons, in the military, and at race tracks, who are trained individuals that can do the telling. These are those who, by the very nature of their calling, have more experience in this area, and are more capable to *"do the work of an evangelist,"* as the apostle Paul tells Timothy in 2 Timothy 4:5. But the command from Jesus to go into all the world was not just limited to His chosen disciples.

First of all, if that were the case, then the Great Commission would have been no longer applicable upon the deaths of those men. This command of Jesus would have been fulfilled.

But secondly, and most importantly, Jesus commanded His disciples to go to all the nations and *make disciples*. Part of that discipling is passing the torch on to the next person to keep the fires of evangelism burning. Part of being discipled is learning how to share one's faith with another individual. Jesus left us no choice in the matter. We *are* to spread the Good News of His salvation. We *are* to bear witness of His love. We *are* to evangelize. When it comes to evangelism, we dare not allow apathy to enter our hearts and keep us from obeying our Lord's command. We cannot push the responsibility off onto those we feel are more qualified. Remember what we mentioned early on in this study. The only qualification required for you to be a witness for Jesus Christ is simply that Jesus has done something for you. This is what you can share with others.

Yet, when we let apathy interfere with our mission for *whatever* reason, we could very likely be preventing that one person God puts in our path from entering His kingdom. There are times when we will feel like sharing this news, and times when we won't. The apostle Paul instructed his son in the ministry in 2 Timothy 4:2, *"Proclaim the word; be prepared in season and out of season."* In referring to this passage, I once heard a preacher say that that means we are to tell the Good News when we feel like it and when we don't feel like it. Even if we may be afraid of offending someone else or "bothering" them, we are still to proclaim the word of salvation to everyone.

Dr. L. R. Scarborough was riding on a train on his way home from an evangelistic crusade. He was tired and weary from a long week of meetings. Sitting across the aisle from him on the train was a gentleman engrossed in his newspaper. Dr. Scarborough said he felt so strongly the pull of the Holy Spirit tugging at the strings of his heart, telling him to share Christ with this stranger. But Dr. Scarborough did not respond to the leading of God's Spirit.

During that forty-five minute ride, the Holy Spirit continued to speak to Dr. Scarborough's heart about this man sitting only a couple of feet from him. But the preacher also continued to choose not to follow the leading of the Spirit even though he knew he should. He rationalized his reasoning by telling himself he was extremely tired, and he really did not want to disturb the man's privacy or offend him. After all, the stranger, too, was probably tired from a long day's work and just wanted to be left alone to relax.

It just so happened that both men were getting off at the same destination. When the train stopped, the stranger stepped off the train ahead of Dr. Scarborough, walked about ten feet, and then collapsed from a fatal heart attack.

Dr. Scarborough was thunderstruck. He moaned and groaned within himself, realizing that God had given him an opportunity to share Jesus with this man and he refused to do so. As he would later describe this incident, he said that he would never know now if this stranger was a Christian. If he had been, what harm would there have been to just speak a word about Jesus? But if he was not a Christian, then he died without Christ and Dr. Scarborough could not help but believe that his blood would be on his hands, because he had the chance to tell this man about the saving power of Jesus, and he let that chance slip through his fingers. All it would have taken would have been just a few minutes of his time. No, maybe the man would not have received the message delivered to him, but at least Dr. Scarborough would have had a free conscience about it. Dr. Scarborough said that from that moment on he never once *ever* failed to share the Good News of salvation with someone again when he felt the Holy Spirit leading him to do so.

I do not believe there are very many of us Christians who can give the same testimony that Paul did in his parting words to the Ephesians in Acts 20:26 when he told them, *"Therefore, I declare to you today that I am innocent of the blood of all men."*

What a testimony! Paul is stating that he never passed up an opportunity to tell others about Jesus. He never allowed anything to stop him from sharing the Good News.

When it comes to evangelism, Paul had what I like to call twenty-twenty vision. In Acts 20:20, he states, *"You know that I have not hesitated to preach anything that would be helpful to you but have taught you publicly and from house to house."* Whether he was speaking publicly to a crowd or one-on-one with individuals, Paul always shared God's Good News. I feel more of us need to have our spiritual eyes examined in order for us to also have twenty-twenty vision.

In the first part of this section I mentioned I do not believe that we, as Christians, develop apathy mainly because we do not care for the souls of others. I repeat, I truly do believe that most of us are genuinely concerned about the lost condition of those without Christ. But if we let this bump in the road of evangelism get in our way, it could possibly mean disaster for someone who does not know Christ as Savior. How do we know that we may not be the very person from whom another one needs to hear about salvation? How do we know that we may not be the one who can get through to a stubborn heart simply because we can relate to, and identify with, that individual's needs at that particular time in his or her life? We must be careful to not let the Good News stop with us.

I mentioned in the first half of this chapter that there was a reason Nineveh just rolled over and died.

Back when Jonah witnessed to the Ninevites and they repented, that particular generation failed to pass it on. Those who had discovered the living God and had embraced and experienced His grace, failed to share the story with the generations that followed. Although they had the responsibility to tell their children, grandchildren, and great-grandchildren about the grace of God, they neglected to do so. We should not be surprised, therefore, that the city died. Neither should we be surprised if some die without Christ because we have failed to pass on the Good News of His saving grace.

Yes, apathy in those to whom we are witnessing, can be very discouraging indeed. There may be no open sin in their lives. Everything may be going well for them, so why should they care about the eternal condition of their souls? So why should we keep trying? We know God has promised us a harvest if we do not faint, but we see no positive results from our efforts. Because of that, if we are not careful, that little mildew of apathy can slowly creep into our minds and hearts and rob us of our desire and the importance of speaking to others about their need for Jesus. But those are the times when we need to learn dependence upon the Lord, and pray more diligently for His guidance and strength so this blight will not fall upon our work.

Whether it is the apathy in the hearts of others or in our own hearts, this bump in the road can stop us dead in our tracks if we let it. In any case, when we confront either side of this bump we need to apply the brakes and stop, look around, get our bearings, and then move forward slowly knowing that on the other side the road will smooth out again...until we arrive at the next bump. This road of evangelism will not *always* be flat. But as long as we remain in the passenger seat and let the Lord continue to drive, we will not be kept from our mission as a result of a flat tire, damaged shock absorbers, harm to the undercarriage, or engine trouble.

CHAPTER 6

MISS THE SIGN…MISS YOUR TURN

I remember as a child our family would take our annual vacation down into Arkansas to spend a week with my maternal grandfather, and then for our second week we would head back up into a very popular Midwestern vacation spot in Missouri simply referred to as Lake of the Ozarks. We always stayed at the same cottage resort area where we could look across the lake at the scenic Bagnell Dam.

Back then—the fifties and early sixties—four-lane highways (we called them double highways) were virtually nonexistent and interstates were probably still something on the Department of Transportation's drawing boards—a thing of the distant future. So, ninety-nine per cent of all our driving from Kansas City and back was done on two-lane highways. Dad did the driving and Mom would sit in the passenger seat with map in hand and do the navigating.

Sometimes we would come across road crews doing construction on the highways. When that happened, oftentimes we would be forced to take a detour, which would make the trip a little longer. Although he never complained about it, Dad would look upon this change in direction as rather an inconvenience. Of course, as kids it never bothered my sister and me sitting in the back seat, along with our dog, Aristotle, whom I mentioned in Chapter 4. Oh yeah. We always took him along. We wouldn't dream of going without him. The detours were never a distraction to the two of us. We would just spend the time playing games, reading, singing songs, or just watching the scenery flash by. We didn't have a care in the world. I remember reading somewhere that "Contentment is enjoying the scenery all along the detour." To this day I can still remember how beautiful it was driving through those Ozark mountains in Missouri and Arkansas….and it is still just as beautiful.

During the week we spent in Arkansas, we would always drive to other locations to visit family members. These side trips often took us deep into the hills of Arkansas to spots you had to look closely on the map to find… if they could even be *found* on the map.

We all know how "country folk" give directions. It's easy for *them* to find their way. They don't need any road signs nor directional signs. Ask them how to get to a certain destination and they very likely will drawl something like, "Weellll, ya just go down yonder road, an' hang a left at the first fork ya'll come to an' then ya go just 'bout a quarter mile down that there road an' cross over a one-lane bridge (they never *had* two-lane bridges in the country, so why they ever mentioned that, I'll never know), an' then ya hang a right after ya pass the second left...or is it the *third* left?...nuh, nuh, it's the second left alright. Nuh, wait a minute. 'Hey, Jenny! Is it the second left or the third left?' Yeah, Jenny says it's the second left alright. Anyhow, ya'll just hang that there right after the second left an' ya go 'bout another half mile or so 'til ya come to another one-lane bridge that crosses over that there crik (that's "creek" for all you city slickers), an' then ya go 'bout another three quarter mile an' ya'll ull come to a little sign that says, 'Dardanelle ½ mile,' with an arrow pointin' east... that's 'right' for you city folk. Just stay on that there main road an' ya'll ull be there in a jiffy. But keep yer eye out for that there sign, 'cause it's kinda tricky an' it's kinda small an' if'n ya miss it, ya'll be in a heap-a trouble. Why, ya'll be clear in the next county bafore ya know it, an' then ya'll havta just turn aroun' an' come back. Anyhow, just stay on that there main road headin' into Dardanelle an' ya'll be there in a jiffy. From here I'd say it's 'bout ten minutes as the crow flies, but beings that ya'll are drivin', it'll prob'ly take ya'll 'bout twenty minutes or there'bouts. Ya'll drive safe now, ya hear? An' be on the lookout for them critters that happen to get onta the road sometimes. Nice talkin' atcha."

I am sure that those of you who have ever done any driving at all in the country in unfamiliar locations know what I am talking about. "Ya'll" been there, done that, right?

By the same token, when we would have to take detours on our vacation, we had to keep an eye out for the correct signs pointing us in the right direction. If we missed the sign, we would miss our turn. And sometimes that would mean going a long distance out of our way because that was the only opportunity we had to go in the right direction. There would be no place along the road to turn around and go back. We would have missed our chance to do the right thing.

In evangelism, we need to be on the lookout for signs which will point us in the right direction, which will point us to the right persons.

Sometimes there may be only *one* sign, and if we miss that sign, we will miss our opportunity.

In the previous chapter we mentioned that the apostle Paul declared, *"I am innocent of the blood of all men"* (Acts 20:26). Paul never passed up an opportunity to share the Good News with others, whether it was publicly or just talking with a single individual. In like manner, Jesus also took advantage of every opportunity He had to share with people. So should we. It was often impromptu, *"by-the-way"* witnessing. It was unpremeditated. As Jesus would travel throughout the countryside, if an opportunity presented itself, He would reach out and seize it. Dr. L.R. Scarborough once said about Jesus' ministry: "He was a mountain-side, wayside, well-side, open-air preacher. He was a highway and hedgeway preacher."

That reminds me of one of the songs we as a family would always sing on those vacation trips to Arkansas:

> *"In the highways, in the hedges,*
> *In the highways, in the hedges,*
> *In the highways, in the hedges,*
> *I'll be somewhere a-workin' for my Lord."*

Some opportunities to witness only pass our way once. We dare not believe that history always repeats itself. The only time we have to evangelize our world is the *"now"* time. The apostle Paul writes in 2 Corinthians

6:2, *"Behold, <u>now</u> is the accepted time; behold <u>now</u> is the day of salvation"* (KJV). There is a certain "todayness" in the Bible which should encourage us to be more realistic about the opportunites God gives us to witness.

This priniciple asks us a question which we need to answer: "If not now, then when?" If we do not seize the natural, normal opportunities which God gives us to share Christ almost every day of our lives when, if ever, *will* we? As we stated in the opening paragraphs of this study, evangelism is not so much wherever you find it, but more properly, it is wherever you *want* to find it.

Before she died, Marilyn Monroe was heard to say, "I don't think anybody cares for me."

Several years ago a man was found dead in a large southern city, one Christmas. The man was more than a week overdue with his rent. So they broke into his room to see what had happened to him. He had been dead for about ten days. Nobody had missed him. There were no clothes in his apartment, not even one additional change of garments. He had lived in that one room in abject poverty. No food, no clothes, emaciated. There was a note scribbled on a torn paper bag. Written with a pencil it said, "Nobody loves me. Nobody lo..." That was the last word he said to this world.

Stop for a moment and try to wrap your mind around such hopelessness. It happened in a city with many churches and great southern hospitality. It might have happened in your city or mine. The tragedy is that it did happen...and it continues to happen almost every day all across this country.

God loved that man. But God's people did not personify that love so that the man could experience it and know it. The type of love, *agape* love, that Jesus demonstrated, and that we are to also show, is meeting the needs of persons. In His evangelism, Jesus met people at their point of need. He could be found at the place of their greatest need. We, too, need to meet people at their point of need; and the first and most important need is salvation.

In John 5:1-18, we read the familiar story of Jesus healing the crippled man at the pool of Bethesda. This place where there were multitudes of invalids, blind, lame, and paralyzed. It was not a pretty sight. How pitiful they all must have been. I am sure that the odors were unpleasant and foul. We are not told of the moanings and groanings, which must have been very audible. Nevertheless, we can only imagine that they were more than sensitive ears and compassionate hearts could bear.

No one is beyond the reach of Jesus' helping hand. Of all the cases at this pool, it is possible that Jesus selected the most difficult one. After all, this man had been paralyzed for thirty-eight years!

In verse 6, Jesus asked this man what initially appears to be a strange question: *"Do you want to get well?"* We immediately want to respond, "What a foolish question." But not necessarily.

Did you ever stop to think that some people enjoy being crippled? Some enjoy the sins of the flesh so much they really and truly do not want to have the radical surgery which Christ requires.

Like an addiction that controls an individual, when it comes to salvation, "want to" is also necessary as that first step down the road to recovery. A decision of the will is involved. Some people may not be whole because they do not *want* to be whole. There are those who rather enjoy their incapacities, their weaknesses, their incompleteness. Why do you think that is?

We have to realize that there are some people who have become so accustomed to others waiting on them and doing for them, that they do not want to make a change. Some enjoy their sinful lifestyle so much they do not want to give it up.

I remember a prison counselor once telling me that one of the reasons there are so many repeat offenders is because when the person gets released from prison, he simply does not know how to cope with the drastic change in his circumstances. Now he has to do for himself in virtually every area of his life. He became so used to having essentially everything done *for* him while on the "inside" that he just cannot make the required adjustments to survive on the outside.

Self-will is vital to evangelism. To be saved, one must exercise his will as well as his emotions. So, this question by Jesus is no idle, unimportant question. It is central and all-important. Jesus will never save anyone who does not *want* to be saved. Even though a person may not be interested in the message we bring, and may not want it, we will never meet a man or woman who does not need what Jesus has to offer.

It is very possible that Jesus may never have passed that way again in His ministry. Jesus took advantage of this opportunity. We read that *"When Jesus saw him lying there and learned that he had been in this condition for a long time, he asked him, 'Do you want to get well?'"* (verse 6). Two things immediately jump out to me in this verse.

First of all, we do not see that this man called out to Jesus to help him as was the case in many of the other healing incidents in Jesus' ministry. We read in the gospels that at any given moment, Jesus could be walking along the road and a leper, or blind man, or someone else would call out to Him to help them in their hopeless condition.

However, we do not read that that was the case here. We read that Jesus was just walking by and saw this man. Jesus saw the sign here and took advantage of an ideal situation. He reached out to this crippled man in his need. Likewise, we, too, need to be looking for those signs all along this road of evangelism to point us to individuals who are waiting for the moving of the waters so they can be healed of the hopeless and helpless condition in which they find themselves. And there may only be one sign. If we miss that sign, we will miss our turn at sharing the solution to their problem, and, unfortunately, that could possibly be the only chance they will ever have to be placed into the healing waters of God's salvation.

The second thing I notice is that *"when Jesus learned"* of his condition He reached out to minister to him. Even though in His divine perceptiveness Jesus very likely knew what was wrong with this man, the very thought that Jesus "learned" of his illness seems to imply that Jesus inquired about this helpless individual. He took the time to find out what this person needed, and how long he had had this need. That begs the question, how often do we, as Christians, take the time to find out about the spiritual conditon of those whom we know?

Or even those we *don't* know, come to think of it? It goes back to the stoplight of "concern" which we discussed earlier in our study. How concerned *are* we...really? Concerned enough to look for that sign along the road? Or, for that matter, are we concerned and perceptive enough to *see* the sign even when we are *not* looking for it?

One of the things which always impressed me about Billy Graham's crusades is that he would close every televised meeting, by looking into the camera and addressing the viewing audience by saying, "And be sure to go to church next Sunday." Did that statement encourage someone to be in church on Sunday? Maybe. Maybe not. But I cannot help but believe that some people—even non church-goers—would possibly attend a church service somewhere as a result of Mr. Graham's request. With that simple statement, he was planting a seed.

Whenever my father would go to the store, upon leaving he would always ask the cashier at the check out stand, "Do you have to work on

Sunday?" If the answer was no, he would always reply in the friendliest, most caring manner, "Be sure to go to church if you can." Did that statement encourage the individual to attend God's House the next Sunday? Maybe. Maybe not. But Dad was planting a thought of encouragement in the person's mind; and if by doing so, just one individual had a life-transforming experience with Jesus Christ, then there would be rejoicing in heaven over the salvation of one soul.

When I was pastoring a church and we would go to a restaurant for a "sit-down" meal where the server would take our order and bring our meal to us I would always try to leave an unspoken word about Christ. When I left the tip on the table, I would leave the bills wrapped around a gospel tract with my business card tucked inside…even if we were eating out of town. My thinking was that you just never know if that one little gesture might be the one thing that person needs in his or her life at that particular time. If not then, perhaps sometime later down the road. If by chance they might be looking for a church home or see a need in their lives to go to church, maybe that would be the encouragement they needed. I am happy to say that as a result of that, two families did start attending our church on a regular basis.

But how about all those others who received those tracts? Did it encourage anyone else to look differently at their lives and their need to have a relationship with Jesus Christ? Maybe. Maybe not. But the point is we never know how the slightest, smallest act of kindness and concern could possibly have a positive, lasting effect upon the recipient.

I remember hearing about a woman who had her own business. She and an employee of hers were driving in the owner's vehicle to a gathering. In the CD player was a CD of one of the owner's favorite Christian artists. She had it turned down low, so they would not have to try to talk above the music. No comment was made by either one about the music that was playing.

After they had been at the social event for a while, the employee needed to leave to go get something. Her employer told her she could take her car. This happened to be on a Sunday.

The next day at work, the employee said to her employer, "You know I really enjoy that music."

Not sure what she was referring to, her boss asked, "What are you talking about?"

The woman replied, "That CD you had playing in your car yesterday. I turned it up and listened to it while I was driving yesterday. You know, he really makes you stop and think."

Her employer told her, "Well, if you really like the music and you want me to, I have some other CD's of his that I can burn for you, so you can have your own copies." To which the woman said she would really like that.

A couple of mornings later after the employee had been given her own copies, the owner walked into the store and heard this music by the Christian artist playing.

The employee said, "I hope you don't mind me playing this, but I really do enjoy this music. But I'll stop playing it if you'd rather I not."

Her boss told her not at all. She could play it as much as she wanted to.

My understanding is that the woman had been dealing with some troubling issues in her family and the owner had encouraged her to think about attending church somewhere, and even recommended the church she herself was attending.

Who knows but that this troubled woman may have needed to hear a message of Good News, regardless of what form it came in, at that particular time in her life? That's not to say this would make her problems go away. But it could possibly help her deal with the emotional stress she was facing. Will this perhaps make a positive, lasting change in this woman's life? Maybe. Maybe not. But this business owner just happened to see a sign on the road which pointed in the direction of someone who was hurting.

Folks, you just never know how the smallest, loving gesture, or act of kindness might be the catalyst to steer another person in the right direction toward salvation and peace with God.

One last thing in John's description of this incident in the life of Jesus, I feel, needs to be seriously addressed.

In verse 7, we read this cripple's reply to Jesus' question: *"Sir, I have no one to help me into the pool when the water is stirred. While I am trying to get in, someone else goes down ahead of me."*

In that tragic statement we see the importance of friends in evangelism. This man had no friend to put him in the water. Many people can never get to Jesus without the help of friends. The healing waters are waiting, but some will never be touched by them unless some friend helps them to Jesus. There is no such thing as a sinner who does not need a friend. Friends are exceedingly important in evangelism.

My evangelism professor, Dr. Miles, once stated, "Let us learn to befriend those who have everything *but* friends, and those who have nothing *including* friends, in order to introduce them all to Jesus, *our* friend, who is a friend to the friendless."

Jesus asked this man a very pertinent question. A question that demands an answer.

As bringers of the Good News, we need to realize that evangelism is costly. As we witness to those who are in need of salvation, we may need to speak more about the demands of the Gospel.

What does the Good News demand? It demands a response: A yes or no; acceptance or rejection. It demands repentance: A revolutionary change in persons. It demands a profound change in lifestyle. It demands we become faithful disciples of Christ.

In other words, when Jesus saves us, He does not let it go at that. There is more to our being saved than just simply praying the sinner's prayer, and walking away…and that needs to be made clear to new converts.

How long have you been a Christian? Do you continually make a concerted effort to go beyond just your conversion experience? Have you made an effort to reach out to those who are crippled in their sin and rebellion?

If we are sincere about our evangelism, we need to make a definite, conscientious effort to look for signs along the road which will point us toward those who are searching for the right direction in their lives. Sometimes those signs will be very obvious. At other times, they will not be so apparent. The signs could be as plain as an open, blatant life of sin; or some type of addiction, whether it be drugs, alcohol, gambling, lying, cheating, stealing, sex, anger, or a tendency toward physical abuse of others. Quite often, these signs can be as clearly seen as a cripple lying by a pool waiting for someone to place him in the way of healing.

But far too often, the signs we need to see may not be so clear to the naked eye. *Those* signs may be hidden behind an overgown tree of deceit, mental abuse, sex or spousal abuse, manipulation, greed, avarice, or the lust for power. Or they may be buried deep in the ditch of depression, despondency, heartbreak, low self esteem, a feeling of complete inadequacy and unworthiness, or a destructive sense of not being loved as was the case of Marilyn Monroe and the man found dead in his apartment whom we mentioned at the beginning of this chapter.

Regardless of the situation, each of these deep-seated crises is just as important to one of those individuals as the other. And it is important to God.

And it is important to Jesus Christ. And it *certainly* should be important to everyone of us.

We need to be in tune with God's Holy Spirit so He can open our eyes and ears and hearts to the signs of pain, hurt, loss, heartbreak, and suffering that plagues persons all around us. If we make it a serious matter of prayer, and if we allow Him, God will help us see these needs in individuals wherever we are, and He will open the door of opportunity for us to be a friend to the friendless, to help the cripples walk, the blind see, the deaf hear, and the unloved to feel love.

All along this road of evangelism we are going to come across signs pointing us in the direction we need to go to reach others with the saving knowledge of Jesus Christ. They are hurting and lost and dying. And we could possibly be the only road map they will ever have. But we need to keep our "eye out for that there sign, 'cause it's kinda tricky an' [sometimes] it's kinda small an' if'n [we] miss it, [we'll] be in a heap-a trouble." And so will that person who needs to find direction for his or her life. My friends, let us be extra careful traveling down this road. We don't want to miss that sign God has placed there for us, because if we miss the sign, we will miss our turn.

CHAPTER 7

THE IMPORTANCE OF BEING A FLAGGER

*A*ll across our country when we drive down streets, highways, and interstates, it is not uncommon for us to come upon road construction. Invariably, as we are approaching the construction site, we will see one of those orange, diamond-shaped signs with black trim and lettering which simply reads, "Flagger Ahead." When we see that sign, we know that up ahead there will be a man or woman standing at the beginning of the work area, holding an orange flag directing us to either slow down, move over one lane, or to just stop momentarily while the road crew is doing its work.

I may be wrong, but I would venture to say that the job of a flag person is possibly one of the most unenviable, unappreciated, and least sought-after jobs anywhere. Think about it for a moment. Those individuals are required to stand out in all kinds of weather, all year round, all hours of the day and night, patiently directing traffic to make sure no accidents occur, the construction workers remain safe while doing their work, and to minimize as much as possible the inevitable traffic snarls. Yes, it is a thankless job, but like the saying goes, "*Somebody's* gotta do it." And you know what? I am grateful for those numerous, nameless "somebodies" who help point us drivers in the right direction. If it were not for the flaggers, did you ever stop to think how chaotic it might be when we approached these construction areas with no one there to show us the way we needed to go, and in which lane we needed to be driving? How often do we drive past these individuals and never give them a second thought? Quite the contrary, too often we possibly may be grumbling something unpleasant as we drive by, thinking only of the inconvenience it is causing us in getting to our desired destination.

To demonstrate how ignorant I was regarding this type of work, I read a newspaper article some time ago that there were actually schools of training for these individuals to attend to ensure that they knew what they were doing once they got out there on the job. Like most other people, I'm sure, I was unaware of just how much is involved in learning how to do the job of a flag person. I just never gave it any thought. I just assumed it was a matter of applying for the job, the employer hires you, and then tells you to report to work at a certain time and you will be given a flag to wave at traffic, or a stick with a sign on it indicating to the oncoming drivers that they need to slow down or stop. But that is not the case at all.

These men and women alongside the road holding flags and signs really do need to know what they are doing. There is more to it than meets the eye. And, yet, all that they are taught and trained to do boils down to essentially only one purpose: To point travelers on the road in the right direction.

When it comes to evangelism we have one initial purpose, and one purpose only. We are to point others to the salvation they can only find in Jesus Christ. We are to make sure they stay in the correct lane to avoid any snarls that would result in serious traffic jams on their road to eternity. We are to be the men and women on this road of evangelism holding our caution flags to direct travelers through the construction sites of their lives so they will safely arrive at the intended destination God has planned for all His children.

In the gospel of John, chapter four, we read the very familiar story of Jesus and "the woman at the well." This is probably the most often used incident in evangelism. The case of this woman's conversion has very likely been used by more writers as a model of evangelism than any other story. More gold on evangelism can be mined from this case than even from the case of Nicodemus in John, chapter 3.

John 4:4-42 may be the single most abundant passage on witnessing in the whole Bible. We see Jesus at His best in John 4. Although tired and weary, we see Jesus taking time to spend with one hopelessly lost woman. His basic way was one-on-one. The Lord majored in one-on-one evangelism. He took time to address this woman's needs and win her to God's grace. When was the last time you personally won anyone to Jesus? When was the last time you tried?

When it comes to speaking one-on-one to persons about Jesus Christ, a common and not insignificant concern of a lot of people is that they would not know what to say or how to approach the subject. That is understandable, especially for those new in the faith or for those who have never been comfortable talking to other people about almost *anything*, let alone their need for Christ in their lives.

In Matthew 10:19-20, Jesus gives us a promise. He says, *"Do not worry about what to say or how to say it. At that time you will be given what to say, for it will not be you speaking, but the Spirit of your Father speaking through you."* If we are to be able to say the right thing at the right time to the right person, we need to ask for God's help and guidance. Jesus said, "Ask and it will be given to you...For everyone who asks receives." Do you need help trying to find the right words to say at the right time? Do you need help knowing when that right time is? Jesus said all we need do is ask and it will be given to us.

This is when our prayer time in evangelism becomes so crucial. We need to be constantly praying to God for His help and strength and power to give us the right words at the right time. Prayer is vital in evangelism. Without the power of prayer we are helpless in this battle against Satan for lost souls. We need to bathe ourselves and those to whom we are witnessing in continual prayer. We need to be continually seeking the guidance of God's Holy Spirit in our evangelism.

In Luke 11:1, we read, *"One day Jesus was praying in a certain place. When he finished, one of his disciples said to him, 'Lord, teach us to pray.'"* Do you see the powerful significance in that question? Jesus did not teach us how to preach. He did not teach us how to sing. He taught us how to *pray*. Jesus' entire ministry was empowered by prayer. If Jesus, the very Son of God, thought prayer was vitally important to Him, how much more so should it be important to us?

The opening verse in this incident of Jesus and the Samaritan woman states, *"Now he had to go through Samaria"* (John 4:4).

Samaria was a region which all Jews avoided like the plague, so much so that sometimes in order to get from one place to another, some Jews would circumvent Samaria altogether, adding as much as two or three hours—or even more—to their time of travel. Yet Jesus "had to go through Samaria." Why?

On the surface, the answer to that question may be as simple as the fact that Samaria just happened to be on their way…in their direction of travel. So, why *not* go through Samaria? That could very easily be the reason Jesus and His disciples "had to go through Samaria." I do not want to be guilty of disallowing altogether the possibility that, literally speaking, that was the reason Jesus needed to go through Samaria. I do not want to fall into the trap of only spiritualizing this statement and eliminating entirely the literal translation here. However, as I study this statement more closely two points prevent me from accepting this as nothing more than Samaria just "being on their way" while traveling.

First of all, the Greek word used to indicate Jesus' need to go through Samaria, is the word, *"dei."* It is a word that means it was "needful" for Jesus to travel through Samaria. Not the kind of "needful," meaning the quickest and shortest route to His destination. It was "imperative" that Jesus go this way. It is the "needful" which means it "behooved" Him to do so. It means this was a necessity in reference to what is required to attain some end; and Jesus had a very particular end in sight. Jesus, in His wisdom, knew there was someone in this city of Sychar who was going to need to hear what He had to say. There was someone who needed to be pointed in the right direction.

But, secondly, the text specifically states that *He* had to go through Samaria. It does not say that *they* needed to, or that He and His disciples needed to. It very clearly mentions Jesus was the one who needed to take this road. Jesus had to go through Samaria so He could give the water of life to this woman, who in turn would share it with the townspeople.

Read what happened because of this woman's testimony: *"Many of the Samaritans from that town believed in him because of the woman's testimony, 'He told me everything I ever did'"* (vs. 39). We read further that when they listened to Jesus, *"Because of his words many more became believers"* (vs. 41). And then in verse 42, the people of the town tell the woman, *"We no longer believe just because of what you said; now we have heard for ourselves, and we know that this man really is the Savior of the world."*

Jesus *had* to go through Samaria. If He had not done so, look at all the souls that would never have seen the flag of caution being waved at them, telling them to slow down and change lanes thereby putting them on the correct path to everlasting life. Jesus had to go through Samaria because He needed to make Himself available to this woman and the city residents. Remember what we said earlier. God is not so much interested in our *ability* as He is in our *availability*. If we make ourselves available, He *will* use us. How available have you made yourself lately to those in need of Jesus? Once you are available, do you truly believe strongly enough in the message you are bringing to convince others how important salvation is in their lives? Sam Schumaker once stated, "If we can't talk convincingly to others about Jesus, what real good are we to them? What real good are we to Him?"

As we examine this interview Jesus had with this woman, we see how He was able to convince her of her need for God's grace. He knew this was a matter of life and death for her. We should be just as convinced in our witnessing as Jesus was.

Don't misunderstand what I am saying. We can be truly convinced in our hearts and to the very depths of our souls about the truth of our message, and, yet, still see people walk away from us without Christ in their lives. Let me repeat what I said earlier. We are engaged in spiritual warfare and not every battle we fight will be won. That does not mean we did not believe with our heart, soul, and mind that what we were sharing was the truth. What I *am* saying is that if we are not sincerely convinced of our message, others could very likely see through that veneer of insincerity. If we do not have a passion for souls, we will not go looking for them.

In this incident in the life of Jesus, a very important aspect of evangelism almost jumps off the page at me. Notice that while this woman's sex life was on par with Hollywood today, Jesus does not lecture her on her sexual sins. The content of His message did not stoop to such condemnation and abuse. Jesus was not a negative preacher who sought to tear others down. By the same token, also please note that He never *once* asked her to change her lifestyle. Jesus did not stand in judgment of her...although as God, He would have had that right. That's not what He was there for.

That reminds me of the incident later in John, chapter 8, about the woman caught in the act of adultery. The religious leaders brought her to Jesus to see if He would obey the law of Moses and agree that she be stoned. We know Jesus' immortal answer to their question: *"If any one of you is without sin, let him be the first to throw a stone at her"* (vs. 7). Think about Jesus' love for this woman. Because of His sinlessness, the very person who had a right to do what He just told the others to do, refused to pick up a stone. Jesus did not come here to judge us. He came here to save.

Yes, Jesus did let the Samaritan woman know He knew all about her sexual looseness and failures, but that was not the major thrust of His message. Jesus did not point out to her all her faults. Neither are we to stand in judgment of others. That is not our job. Our job is to fish, not clean up the fish bowl. Allow me to expand on that statement briefly.

When we are witnessing to others about Christ, we are not to read people a long list of rules of spirituality en route to salvation. We are to present to them the Savior. We are to press the issue of their relationship to the Lord Jesus. I repeat, our job is not to clean up the fish bowl, certainly not initially. Our job is to fish—just fish. God will take care of all the rest.

Not only was this woman a hated Samaritan, but she was also a lowly prostitute. Yet, Jesus did not hesitate to talk with this woman because she was a Samaritan prostitute. We need to ask ourselves the question, "How on earth shall we convert real sinners to Jesus Christ if we refuse to come into contact with them?" If we are to pattern our evangelism after that of Jesus, we will show the same respect for personality as He did. The very first issue which we must settle is our attitude toward persons. If we do not believe individuals are worth saving, we will not lift so much as one finger to save them. If we truly respect personality, we shall ascribe infinite worth to *every* human being.

A flagger alongside the road is concerned about the safety of the drivers as well as the construction crew. That is what they are there for. They want to make sure the drivers are heading in the right direction. Yes, perhaps to some of them it may be "just a job." But I cannot help but believe that, being human, they would feel a sense of sorrow if a driver ended up getting hurt because he did not follow the directions of the flag person. And I am certain that the flaggers themselves would feel a sense of sorrow if, due to their negligence or lack of commitment to their task, someone was injured, or worse, killed.

Likewise, in evangelism we need to feel a deep sorrow for those who are lost. The apostle Paul writes in Romans 9:2-3, *"I have great sorrow and unceasing anguish in my heart...for the sake of my brothers, those of my own race."* Folks, if we do not feel sorrow in our heart over the fate of those who are spiritually lost, then we do not see the world as God sees it. Witnessing for Christ will be effective only when words of truth come from a heart of compassion.

After this discourse with the Master, we read in verses 28-29 that *"leaving her water jar, the woman went back to the town and said, 'Come, see a man who told me everything I ever did. Could this be the Christ?'"* This woman completely forgot her purpose for coming to the well in the first place. What need did she have for physical water at that moment? She had just been given the Water of Life! She had just experienced inside her *"a spring of water welling up to eternal life"* (vs. 14). She had been given new purpose and new direction for her life.

This woman was on a mission. She now had a message to share. She had experienced a new road to travel. I can almost see her running back into her town, not caring what others had ever thought of her before, nor caring what they thought now, waving her arms—maybe waving her *own* flag—inviting others, "Come, see a man!"

When this woman awoke that morning, everything was as it had always been. She was the same lowly, despised Samaritan prostitute who always kept to herself. The same woman who would go to the well to draw water in the middle of the day, rather than in the morning or evening when all the other women went, just so she could avoid the insulting remarks and offensive, hateful stares she would receive from them. The same woman whose only purpose in life was to make a living by selling her body to the next man who came along. This was that same woman. But now she had a message. What a metamorphosis!

My friends, that is *our* message. "Come, see a man!" Come, and experience a complete transformation in your life. Come, and partake of the Water of Life. Come, and know the love of a great God who loves you just as you are, scars and all. Come, and talk to a Savior who will accept you right now without judging you, or asking you to clean up your act first.

Certainly, we are going to meet skeptics along this road of evangelism. That is one of those unavoidable bumps. When the townspeople went out to see for themselves what this woman was talking about, considering the bringer of this news, I am sure the majority of them were very skeptical; but their curiosity got the best of them and they followed her lead. I am sure many of the people, when they heard what the woman had to say, probably said in return, "Yeah, right! Come on! We're supposed to believe *you*?" Can't you just hear them? But that is the way of our human nature. So, in reply, the woman simply said, "Well, if you don't want to believe *me*, then come see for yourself, and make up your own minds. Come, see a man!"

All the arguments in the world; all the attempts at persuasion and convincing; all the rationalization you can use; all the scripture verses you quote; all the transformation that is seen in your life, may never encourage some individuals to embrace Christ as their Savior. They are just going to have to experience it themselves. But by that same token, they will never experience it if we don't do our part. If we are not that flag person directing them into the correct lane, they will never know which way to go.

In the first chapter of John's gospel, verses 35-51, we see the calling of Jesus' first disciples. One day John the Baptist saw Jesus walking by, and pointed Him out to two of his disciples: Andrew and probably John, although John's name is not mentioned. John and Andrew followed Jesus. They asked Him where He was staying, and He replied, *"Come, and you will see"* (vs. 39).

Later, Andrew found his brother, Simon Peter, and told him, *"We have found the Messiah"* (vs. 41). Andrew brought Peter to Jesus. He told Peter, "Come, and see." We read in the subsequent verses that Jesus found Philip and told Philip to follow Him. Then Philip found Nathanael and told him, *"We have found the one Moses wrote about in the Law, and about whom the prophets also wrote—Jesus of Nazareth, the son of Joseph"* (vs. 45). To which Nathanael replied, *"Nazareth! Can anything good come from there?"* (vs. 46). Nazareth was a small, insignificant, out-of-the-way village that really did not have much going for it. (In taking a tour of Judea, Nazareth was not one of the favorite stops along the way). In responding to Nathanael's question, what did Philip say? He just simply said, "Come and see. If you don't believe me, Nathanael, come and see for yourself."

The Samaritan woman told the townspeople, "Come and see." Jesus told John and Andrew, "Come and see." Andrew told Peter, "Come and see." Philip told Nathanael, "Come and see." The pattern here is unmistakable. If others are to know Jesus as the One who came to seek and to save those who were lost, we need to invite them to come and see for themselves. We need to wave them in the right direction.

In John 4:35-36, Jesus tells His disciples, *"Open your eyes and look at the fields! They are ripe for harvest. Even now the reaper draws his wages, even now he harvests the crop for eternal life, so that the sower and the reaper may be glad together."*

This incident of the Samaritan woman shows the connection between sowing and reaping in evangelism. Sowing and reaping are intimately tied together in evangelism. Unless someone sows there will be nothing to reap. He who sows will eventually reap. If by chance the sower and the reaper are different persons, they can still rejoice together because the fruit has been gathered. This incident includes both sowing and reaping. It magnifies both sowing and reaping.

After pastoring a church for several years, my father left to take another pastorate, leaving many friends and fond memories behind him. When the next pastor of that church came on board, it became a rather eye-opening and educational experience for my sister, who had seen our father labor so diligently and faithfully in that community's harvest field.

I guess you might say there was a personality clash between my sister and the new pastor. She still attended faithfully, and still served in the church. But there were a few issues with the direction the new ministry was going which rubbed my sister the wrong way.

Within the first several months of the new pastor's tenure, a number of souls were coming to know Christ as their Savior, as well as a number of new additions to the church, many of whom Dad had ministered to for years, with very little or no results...except negative results. Well, that just didn't set too well with my sister, not that she became angry over it, or copped an attitude, or anything of that nature. It just disturbed her to see so many people whom Dad had witnessed to, worked with, prayed over, and cried over, for so many years, now coming to salvation under this other pastor's ministry. She felt that the right person was not getting the credit for a "job well done."

When she confessed her feelings to Dad one day during a visit, in that fatherly way of his he said, "Now, now, Jo, you don't want to have that kind of attitude. I served the Lord as faithfully as I knew how while I was there. He let me know that my work there was finished. Someone else has come along to take up the mantle. While I was there my purpose for many of those people was to, obviously, simply plant the seed. Someone else has come along to water that seed. But it is *God* who has given the increase, and I can't help but rejoice because of it. All the credit and glory belongs to Him. I sowed the seed. Someone else watered that seed. But God is the One who produced the fruit, and *that* is the important thing for you to remember." Sis never forgot that lesson, and it gave her a new perspective.

One sows. Another reaps.

Jesus told His disciples in verse 38, *"I sent you to reap what you have not worked for. Others have done the hard work, and you have reaped the benefits of their labor."* Look at those three words that are frequently overlooked in this passage: "I sent you."

Jesus has appointed us to this task of laboring in His vineyard. He has commanded us to be the flaggers pointing others down the road that leads to everlasting life. We may be doing many things and doing them well. But we are not fulfilling His appointment for us unless we are engaged in ministry in the harvest field.

Sowing and reaping. The Lord has appointed us to this. He sends us to labor in the harvest. That harvest can be anywhere we want it to be. Every time the Lord gives us an opportunity to say a word for Him, we need to take advantage of that opportunity. Call somebody. Visit somebody. Invite somebody. Bring somebody. Tell them what God has done for you. Demonstrate the love of God in Jesus. Pray for them. If nothing else, you can at least do as the woman at the well did: *"Come, see a man."*

How important is your witness? Only eternity will *really* tell. But God wants you to realize its importance today.

Ever heard of a man by the name of Edward Kimball? Probably, most of you would say, "No," unless you are up on your history of the Christian church over the last 150 years or so. But I am sure most of you have heard of a great preacher by the name of Dwight Lyman Moody, or more often referred to as D. L. Moody…the preacher regarded as the "man who shook two continents for Jesus Christ."

When he was seventeen, Moody went to work in his uncle's shoe store in Boston, Massachusetts. His uncle encouraged Moody to attend church. While attending church, Edward Kimball became D. L. Moody's Sunday school teacher.

One day Kimball paid the young Moody a visit at the store, and while the youth was putting away shoes in the back room, he convinced Moody to give his life to Christ. Kimball, who had become aware that he probably did not have long to live, also visited each of the other members of his class and led them to Christ as well.

Years later, when he was preaching in England, Moody, who became one of the great evangelists of all time, was telling this story of Kimball in the church of F. B. Meyer. One of the teachers in the church was so inspired by the story that she told it to her Sunday school class. As a result, each member gave her heart to Christ. This event in Meyer's church revolutionized his ministry.

But not only was Meyer's ministry revolutionized, so was another young minister's through Meyer's preaching. When he was preaching in the United States in Moody's school in Northfield, Massachusetts, Meyer put the emphasis, as he so often did, on the need for consecration. "If you are not willing to give up everything for Christ," Meyer said, "are you willing to be *made* willing?" That shook a young man sitting in the back row, and as a result, his entire ministry was transformed. The man's name was J. Wilbur Chapman. Chapman not only became a great evangelist in his own right, but he became one of the most influential churchmen of his time. He was a leader in the YMCA movement, the first director of the Winona Lake Bible Conference, and a moderator of the Presbyterian general assembly.

Meyer influenced many others as well, including the great Baptist preacher, Robert G. Lee (R. G. Lee), last of the orators in the William Jennings Bryan traditon. Lee was a distraught student at Furman University at the time, but a message by Meyer turned his life around.

But let's go back and trace this evangelistic chain still futher through Chapman.

When Chapman was associated with the YMCA, an organization that Moody and he had effectively breathed new life into, he met a former professional baseball player, now a YMCA clerk. Later, Chapman turned over his ministry in evangelism to this man when he returned to the pastorate. The clerk, whose name was William Sunday, had worked intimately with Chapman in his crusades for two years. Now, through superb organizational skills and sensational preaching, he was able to preach to more than a hundred million during his lifetime, an incredible feat! It is said that as many as a million "hit the trail" through his ministry.

In 1924, Billy Sunday, as he came to be known, preached in Charlotte, North Carolina, and through his preaching there, a layman's group was founded that sought to carry on a witness for Christ in the community. In 1932, they organized a crusade and called Mordecai Ham in to preach.

Ham's preaching was deeply disturbing to one 16-year-old high school senior who sat in the tent night after night. He and his friend, Grady Wilson, thought they could "escape" by sitting behind the preacher in the choir. But such was not to be. Finally, young Billy Graham and his friend,

Grady, went forward to indicate they were ready to begin their life with Christ.

This story as told by James H. Semple in a 1967 article in *Christianity Today*, entitled "Passing the Torch of Evangelism," is one of the most amazing examples of the pyramiding effects of sharing the faith that I have ever come across. And all because an "unknown" Sunday school teacher was concerned enough about a teenage stocker in a shoe store to share the love of Jesus with him.

What is your potential? You have every bit as much potential for the Kingdom of God as Edward Kimball. Why? Because you serve the same God and you share the same love and you lift up the same Jesus that Edward Kimball did. *Never* diminish your importance of being a flagger on this road of evangelism. *Never* underestimate how crucial it is for you to hold that flag of caution for travelers on the highway of life who need to see clearly the lane in which they need to be driving. Your smallest witness can have an immense impact. Your deepest relationship is bound to!

Jesus' disciples did not have much real ability from the world's standpoint. They were not educated. They were not trained in public speaking.

They did not have the right political or religious connections. Yet the Bible says they turned the whole world upside down!

But, you see, Christ was not looking for ability. And His primary interest today is not ability either. It is not your *ability* that matters. It is your *availability*. The roadside flaggers make themselves available to help us avoid injury, harm, and, in some cases, even death.

God wants to use you to accomplish great things for His kingdom. He wants, especially to work through you to win the lost back to Himself. At least six times in the gospel of John, Jesus refers to doing His Father's work, and every time it had redemptive connotations. If we want to accomplish the Father's work, we need to give priority to the redemption of lost people.

Jesus made Himself available to this Samaritan woman. The Samaritan woman ran back into town, waving her flag, making herself available to the townspeople. And look at the result. Look how many were directed off the lane of destruction and onto the road to everlasing life. And all she said was, "Come, see a man!"

Are you available? Are you willing to turn your life over to Him for His use? If you are not willing, are you willing to be *made* willing?

CHAPTER 8

BE ON THE LOOKOUT FOR BLIND SPOTS

Almost every vehicle people drive on our roads today has at least one blind spot, and perhaps more. Regardless of how accurately we adjust our outside mirrors, there is invariably a blind spot where we cannot see another vehicle approaching on either side of us. This "blindness" may only last for a second or two, but we all know that in those brief two seconds a major accident can possibly occur, which could cause serious injury and even death. That is why we have to keep a close eye out for other drivers when we are getting ready to change lanes. We cannot always depend upon what we see in those outside mirrors. We have to carefully look over either shoulder to make sure we are not about to move over into the path of oncoming traffic.

I currently drive a Jeep Wrangler, and I absolutely love it. I have received so much fun and enjoyment from driving that little four-wheel-drive just about everywhere. I especially receive an extra amount of pleasure in nice weather when I can put the top down, and at times, take the doors off, and just truck on down the road, feeling the rush of the wind all around me and through my hair. (Of course, my hair is an absolute mess when I have finally reached my destination...but who cares, right? I certainly don't).

The only major issue I have ever really had with my jeep up to this point is that there are some serious blind spots on both sides of me when I am driving down the road. So serious, that a couple of times I just barely missed pulling over into the next lane that was already occupied by an approaching vehicle. Not that I was being inattentive, I just did not see the other driver in time. I finally had to buy a couple of those little convex stick-on mirrors to place on my outside mirrors to help avoid those blind spots. I had never had to use them before and it has been amazing how much difference they make while driving.

Another type of blind spot along the roadways we travel everyday is the kind which blocks our view from other traffic on the road, or hides the road signs which are put in place to prevent possible accidents. Sometimes, for whatever reason a sign or marker is hidden from view by trees, bushes, or telephone poles; or the sign has been erected in what is not the most strategic location to avoid mishaps. This was brought home in a very tragic way to a state transportation department of one of our nation's highways.

I remember reading how a family of four was driving on a road which intersected a fairly major highway. There was a stop sign at that intersection, but it was not placed in an ideal location and it was mostly hidden by a telephone pole. Not seeing the sign, the father did not stop and kept driving through the intersection. As a result, a tractor trailer truck driving on the highway rammed into the family's passenger car, killing three of the occupants and seriously injuring the fourth. This incident hit the local newspaper, and within days that stop sign was moved to a much more visible location where no driver approaching that intersection could miss seeing it.

Regardless of what area or walk of life we may be discussing, blind spots all too often can lead to tragic, and sometimes, fatal results. In evangelism, we need to be aware that there are some blind spots along the road.

When it comes to evangelism, I feel there may be three types of blindness: The blindness of those to whom we witness who are just blind to the fact that simple faith in some historical man named Jesus can actually make a difference in their lives; the blindness of others who refuse to believe that such a drastic change can take place in those they know who have lived such lives that were so diametrically opposed to a Christian lifestyle; and our own personal blindness to those around us who are in need of the help and the hope we can bring them through Jesus Christ.

In John, chapter 9, we have what I have always felt is one of the most telling witnessing experiences found in the life and ministry of Jesus. This is the familiar story of the man born blind and Jesus heals him. The disciples ask Jesus who sinned, this man or his parents, that he was born blind. This question was asked because it was believed by the people back then that if an individual was born with some kind of physical impairment, then it had to be the result of the parents' sin or the sin of the individual himself.

Jesus answered their question by telling them that it was not the fault of either one's sins. He explained to them that this man was born blind so that the work of God could be seen in his life (vs.3).

Skepticism abounds in the hearts and minds of people all over the world. We live in a very skeptical society. People everywhere refuse to believe certain truths until they see them for themselves; and even then, sometimes, they remain a little doubtful. They still need to be convinced of what they are hearing or seeing. They still feel there may be some kind of trickery or even manipulation involved...maybe even some type of mind control.

When it comes to sharing the message of Jesus' salvation with others, we can be up against the worst kind of skeptic. People so blinded by their rationale and logic-oriented minds that it is absolutely impossible, at times, to convince them, number one, of their need for salvation, and number two, that some guy named Jesus who lived over two thousand years ago can provide that need. It's another one of those major bumps in this road of evangelism.

In the previous chapter we discussed the incident of Jesus and the Samaritan woman from John, chapter four. When this woman began telling others what Jesus had done for her, I am sure they were very skeptical; and from the point of view of our human nature, can we blame them? Such a change in a woman like this? They knew her far too well.

But then she invited these same people to come see this man who could very likely bring about a change in their own lives. What kind of nonsense was this woman spouting? How could just one man be that influential in their lives? So influential that He would cause them to *also* change? I can almost hear them. "Are you crazy, woman? Ain't nobody can do that!" But, nevertheless, she invited them just the same. It's like that old TV commercial where some boys are telling little Mikey to try *Life* cereal, "Try it. You'll like it!"

In this ninth chapter of John where Jesus has restored the sight of the blind man, the Pharisees categorically deny the possibility that Jesus could bring healing to this man. There are at least two reasons for this that I can see.

First of all, these self righteous stuffed shirts were just jealous of Jesus. Plain and simple. They were just…plain…jealous. They absolutely did not like all the attention Jesus was getting from the people. After all, for years these Pharisees had been the religious leaders of the day. The people were to look to *them* for spiritual guidance. And then along comes this *Nazarene*, of all people, who did not have any kind of religious training, taking over the spotlight.

Secondly, they accused Him of being a horrible sinner. He had made clay on the Sabbath! Of all the nerve! This sinner actually "worked" on the Sabbath! (We know this was not the first time Jesus was confronted with this argument from the Pharisees). So, because this man, Jesus, was such a terrible sinner, there is no way that He could have healed the blind man as he testified that Jesus did.

The Pharisees asked the man what Jesus had done to bring about such healing. The man replied, *"He put mud on my eyes, and I washed, and now I see* (vs. 15). It's as simple as that, guys." And the way this story unfolds just makes me want to say to the blind man, "You go, buddy! You tell 'em!"

We read in verse sixteen that some of the Pharisees said, *"This man is not from God, for he does not keep the Sabbath."* But some of the others asked, *"How can a sinner do such miraculous signs?"* This question divided the Pharisees in their opinion.

Let me say right here that Jesus is the great Divider. He divides good and evil, sin and sinlessness, proud and humble, powerful and powerless, just and unjust, Christian and non-Christian; and because of that He can even divide friends and family, governments and nations. When we decide to take a firm stand for Christ we can count on opposition and divisiveness. Jesus Himself said in Matthew 10:34, *"Do not suppose that I have come to bring peace to the earth. I did not come to bring peace, but a sword."* So because of Jesus, even these staunch religious leaders were divided. Eventually, Jesus will cause *everyone* to take a stand either for Him or against Him, if not in this life then in the life to come.

The Pharisees turned to the man again and asked him what he thought of Jesus since it was *his* eyes that were opened. To which the man replied, *"He is a prophet"* (vs. 17).

These proud men still refused to accept the truth of what the man was telling them so they called his parents to ask *them* if he was their son and if he was born blind, and if that was the case, how was he able to now see. I love how the parents responded. They told these Jews that this man was their son and he was indeed born blind. But how he is now able to see, "We don't know. He's old enough to speak for himself. Ask *him*" (vs. 21).

The Pharisees go back and tell the man to give God the glory for his healing because they absolutely knew this man, Jesus, was a sinner, to which the healed man answered with what I have always considered the quintessence of *all* testimonies in verse 25 when he tells them, "Whether He's a sinner or not, I don't know. All I know is that I woke up this morning the same blind man I have been all my life, and *now* I can see. And that man, Jesus, is the one who made it all possible and, fellas, that's good enough for me."

Folks, *that* is our testimony. *That* is our witness. Our witness to others is that "No, I can't explain the trinity. I can't explain how God created the universe. I can't explain the Virgin Birth. I can't explain how faith works. I can't explain any of those "inconsistencies" and "glitches" in the Bible to the satisfaction of those rationalists who like to emphasize such things. I don't know the answers to such questions. But one thing I do know is that for the first time in my sinful, blinded life I can see clearly, and *Jesus* is the one who is responsible, and my life has never been the same since. That's all I need to know."

How do I know Jesus saved my eternal soul one dark night on a back road outside of Wichita, Kansas? Because I was there when it happened.

The Pharisees ask the man again what Jesus did to him to make him see. This man is great! You gotta love him! He answers, "I've already told you what He did, and you didn't listen. Why do you want to hear it again? Do *you* guys want to become His disciples too?" (vs. 27).

Despite the truth staring these Pharisees in the face, they still refused to believe it. When they could not change the man's mind they resorted to insults and criticism. They accused this man of being less than they were because they were disciples of Moses and they knew God spoke to Moses, but they didn't even know where this Jesus came from.

I can almost see the look of bewilderment on this man's face when he says to them in verses 30-33, "I can't believe this! This is just remarkable! You guys are supposed to be the religious leaders for us. You're the ones who are supposed to know all this stuff. You're the ones who are supposed to be setting an example for us, but yet you don't know where He comes from? We know that God doesn't listen to sinners. He listens to the godly man who does His will. Nobody has ever heard of opening the eyes of a man born blind. If this man were not from God, He couldn't do anything." (Obviously, my own paraphrase).

I love this guy! He does not back down. He does not change his story. He will not be intimidated. He just tells the truth as he knows it. *No one* and *nothing* can change his mind. He *knows* what has happened to him. Don't misunderstand what I am saying here. I am not advocating that just because we know we are right about our salvation experience, that we should adopt an arrogant, smug, cockey attitude. That will not get us anywhere. And I do not believe that was the attitude of the blind man.

He was just simply stating the facts as he knew them, and the Pharisees, blinded to the truth, absolutely refused to believe those facts.

My friends, when your eyes are opened, when the blindness is removed, and especially when you begin to tell the story of your journey from blindness to faith in Jesus Christ, hang on! You *will* be met with resistance, and don't be surprised if you encounter the *most* resistance from *religious* people. "Religious" folks are often uncomfortable around authentic people whose lives have been changed by the living Christ.

We see two types of blindness in this incident. We see how some people just could not believe that a man named Jesus could bring about such a drastic change in an individual's life. Many of us, I am sure, have seen that same scenario repeated time and time again. There are those who simply cannot accept the fact that faith in Jesus can make such a difference in a person's life. In their own rational, logical minds, it does not compute. Either that or they do not believe someone as steeped in sin as the Samaritan prostitute or others engaged in sinful lifestyles can ever change. We find that very evident in the life of the apostle Paul.

We read in Acts 9:21, that after his conversion and when he started preaching Jesus in Damascus, *"All those who heard him were astonished and asked, 'Isn't he the man who raised havoc in Jerusalem among those who call on this name? And hasn't he come here to take them as prisoners to the chief priests?'"*

Paul had to pay his dues. He had to earn their respect and prove that Jesus had brought about a tremendous change in this persecutor of the Church. Because of the blatant skepticism of human beings, sometimes certain Christians have to earn a hearing.

One of the best examples I know of in our time regarding this is Chuck Colson, known as the "hatchet man" during the Nixon administration. Here is a man who seemed to have it all: Power, position, prestige. And yet it all came crumbling down almost overnight. When he had his own life-transforming experience with Jesus Christ, the skeptics were everywhere and very vocal. Yet, undeterred, he persevered, and we are all familiar with the enormous work he has done for the cause of Christ.

All along this road of evangelism we will meet those who refute our testimony and the Good News we bring, and who are blinded to the truth of the gospel. They will not believe such a change as the Bible teaches can take place in the lives of people. They will not believe that simple faith in the man, Jesus, can bring about that change. But like the apostle Paul and

Chuck Colson and many others like them, we must not allow such skepticism to deter us from the task before us.

We bring a message of truth and hope to others. They are not required to accept that message nor believe it, but *we* are required to deliver it. Employees are given management directives by their employers. Soldiers are given orders by their superior officers. The reason being, of course, is because those who are in charge believe it is the best course of action. We as Christians have been given our marching orders by our Commander in Chief and He has asked us to follow those orders. But unlike the work force or the military, if we refuse to follow His orders nothing detrimental will happen to us. We will not be fired or court martialed. However, we will miss out on a real blessing of seeing someone else come to know the same joy and peace we have experienced. And also unlike in the secular world, the directive our Manager has given us will never be in error as is sometimes the case in events that take place in the world around us. We can follow His orders to the letter, knowing He will never lead us astray nor will the message we bring become a hindrance or a stumbling block to others.

This blind spot that is so prevalent in so many people around us can cause untold harm and bring about their own spiritual deaths. When we are confronted with these blind spots in our evangelism, it is imperative that we do all we can, empowered by the Holy Spirit, to lovingly point them out to those individuals and help them look around and beyond their blindness in order to see the clear path ahead of them that leads them to everlasting life. They may still choose to remain in their darkness as did the Pharisees, but that is not to prevent us from offering them that convex mirror of God's salvation to help them overcome their blindness.

We have already discussed earlier in this study the third type of blind spot in evangelism, that of being blind to the needs of others. We will not belabor that point here, only to reiterate the importance of always being open to the leading of God's Holy Spirit when He is pointing us to those with whom He wants us to share the Good News. We need to always have our spiritual eyes and ears open so we can see and hear the needs of persons everywhere.

Before we leave this bump of skepticism on our road of evangelism, I want to address another aspect of it, which really is not being "skeptical" so much as it is being "doubtful." I believe there may be a fine line of difference between the two. To do that I want to pull from the pages of scripture the familiar story of Jesus' disciple, Thomas, after the resurrection of our Lord. I would like to act as his attorney and come to the defense of this "doubter."

In studying this disciple of Jesus over the years, I have come to believe that he has been given a raw deal. He has been saddled with a label that has stuck for centuries. To many he has gone down in history as "the doubter." How many times have we heard, or even used, the expression, "Don't be a doubting Thomas." Thomas has been called a skeptic, a rationalist, an empiricist—the one who needed incontrovertible proof before he would be satisfied. He has been seen as the example for all who dismiss the reality of Jesus Christ on the basis of rational arguments. Many people have believed that Thomas was the one disciple who lived as close as you can get to disbelief. But I feel it is time we see him in a different light, more as an example of *all* of us who are, at one time or another, plagued by doubts.

When Jesus was ready to go back to Judea to raise Lazarus, Thomas is the one who said, *"Let us also go, that we may die with him"* (John 11:16). This man was committed and courageous. He was ready to go to the cross for Jesus. Thomas was the kind of guy who, when he gave himself to someone, gave with all his heart. He had sold himself to the Lord—lock, stock, and barrel.

But then Thomas became disillusioned after the death of Jesus. He wanted to draw back to a safe distance, maybe thinking, "I'm not going to get burned again. Next time it's going to take the Rock of Gibralter, someone I can count on to be there for me for all of my life, before I give of myself so completely." That was Thomas. He was convinced that Jesus was the fulfillment of all his dreams. But then his dreams got shattered. The absolute worst thing that *could* have happened *did* happen. He saw Jesus go to the cross. He saw Jesus die. And all of his dreams died with Him. So, in John, chapter 20, when he heard the incredible, unbelievable word of the disciples that Jesus was alive and had appeared to them, Thomas needed proof before he would recommit his life.

Jesus understood Thomas' doubts. He understood Thomas' fears. He helps people like Thomas, and thank God for that, because there are a lot of us around. A week later Jesus appears to the disciples again and the first thing he says is, "Peace" (John 20:26). There is no rebuke, no criticism, no attack on Thomas' character. Just a gentle word of peace and acceptance. Then He shows Thomas His hands and His side and says, "Here, my child, here is your proof." Who would not be impressed with the way Jesus handled this doubter? He met his need. He showed Thomas just what Thomas had required in order to have the strength to go on living for God all the rest of his life.

Don't tell me you have never had doubts like those of Thomas. Wondering if your belief in the Lord Jesus is not just some great exercise in futility. Facing struggles that make it seem as if God is more absent in your life than present. Dealing with disappointments that have led you to question the validity of your relationship with God. And in those doubting moments when the lights have gone out and the pit is so deep and there's nobody around and tomorrow seems bleak, we also are tempted to say, "He'll have to *prove* it to me next time before I could ever trust Him again." And the beauty of it is that He *does*. He does! Again and again He graciously and lovingly proves Himself to us. He comes in like a flood of grace and compassion, and He shows us His hands and He shows us His side. And He says, "Here, my child, here's proof. I *am* alive and I will live *forever*! And I will *never* leave you or forsake you."

You see, this doubt in the heart of Thomas did not have its roots in skepticism so much as it did in the pain and disappointment and disillusionment that Thomas was feeling. He doubted more out of apprehension than anything else. He had been down that road before and this time he was going to proceed with a lot more caution.

In witnessing to others, we will meet those who have difficulty believing not because they are blatant skeptics, but because they have such a sense of unworthiness about themselves. They doubt because they know the kind of person they are. They are thinking, "How is it possible that Jesus could forgive and save someone like *me*, after all I've done? How could *anyone* accept and love a person like *me*?"

The blind spot in the lives of these people is the "impossibility" that such a thing *is* possible when they look at themselves and see the hopeless and helpless wreck they have made of their lives. And they say, "He'll have to prove it to me." And He does. As we demonstrate to them the love of Jesus, as we help them reach out in faith to Him, He does! He showers them with His grace and compassion, and He says, "Here, here is proof." He meets their need and gives them what they asked for.

As we travel this road of evangelism we will meet skeptics, rationalists, and doubters all along the way. There will be those who scoff at our message and try to refute our testimony. There will be those who, in their feeling of unworthiness, doubt the possibility of the cleansing power of

God's love. But that is why it is called grace. No, in and of ourselves, we are *not* worthy of such love, but Jesus saw *something* in each of us that caused Him to give His life for us, *something* that told Him that even though we are not worthy, we *are* worth dying for. That is the message Jesus wants us to proclaim to all the world. Don't let the blind spots of this world's skepticism, rationalism, and unbelief cause you to stray from your lane of sharing the Good News of the forgiveness and love of Jesus. Blind spots abound, but that does not mean we have to let them blind *us* to those around who *are* blind. Let us pray for God's guidance to know when it is time to make mud and apply it to the eyes of those born blind in their sin, and for His strength and courage to keep on keeping on even when we are faced with those who say, "It can't be."

CHAPTER 9

BEWARE THE PARALYSIS OF TRAFFIC JAMS

We all have run into traffic jams while traveling our nation's roadways. They can be caused by auto accidents, road construction, flooding, serious damages in the pavement, a bridge being out, or any number of reasons. When we are stuck in one of these inevitable inconveniences, a lot of the time there is nothing we can do but wait it out. At such times the highway becomes one long, continuous parking lot.

The worst such case I ever read about happened in a mountain range when a heavily-traveled highway through the mountains became impassable in both directions due to a bridge suddenly needing immediate repairs because of an accident involving a big eighteen-wheeler whose brakes failed, causing the rig to ram into one of the bridge's sides. Fortunately, no one was hurt, but the damage to the bridge made it too dangerous for traffic to drive across it. Before word of the problem could be communicated soon enough to the drivers in the area, the situation had caused a major back up for almost ten miles in both directions, which lasted almost six hours.

What made this even worse is that one side of the highway butted right up against the mountainside with no shoulder. The other side of the four-lane highway had barely a couple of feet separating it from the guardrail constructed next to the mountain's edge which overlooked a sheer, precarious drop of several hundred feet. The usual concrete, dividing wall was all that separated the four lanes of road from each other. There was literally no way for the drivers to turn around and go back the way they had come. They were completely immobilized. The drivers were hopelessly paralyzed where they sat, with no remedy immediately in sight. Perhaps, the only up side of that whole crisis was that it was pleasant weather and the drivers could, at least, get out and stretch their legs while waiting.

On the road of evangelism there are times when we will run into traffic jams which could stop our evangelistic efforts dead in their tracks…if we allow it. We need to beware of such dangers when they confront us. If we are not, it could prevent some lost soul from crossing that bridge which spans that great chasm between a life of everlasting hopelessness and the life of everlasting joy found in Jesus.

Sadly enough, the traffic jams in evangelism are all too often created by well-intentioned Christians who are anxious to get close to Jesus, and are hungry to learn more about Him. As paradoxical as that may sound, I am afraid that, unfortunately, that is the case. There is an incident in the healing ministry of Jesus which, I feel, brings that truth to light all too clearly.

In Mark 2:1-12, we read the familiar story of the paralyzed man brought to Jesus by four friends who, when they could not get into the house to see the Master because of the huge crowds of people, resorted to innovative methods to reach Him, by tearing a hole in the roof of the house, and then lowering their sick friend down to Jesus for healing. You might say they were "raising the roof" in evangelism.

Verse 2 states, *"So many had gathered that there was no room left, not even outside the door."* It was wall-to-wall people inside, and extending several feet outside the door and probably snaking around the sides of the house. Wherever Jesus is, He can attract a crowd. But sometimes that crowd can keep certain other individuals from coming to Jesus. Those who are healthy will sometimes prevent the sick from getting to Jesus. Those who are whole do not need the touch of this Great Physician's hand as much as those who are sick.

I remember reading somewhere that Soren Kierkegaard spoke of "the individual" over against "the masses," "the one" over against "the many." "The many" sometimes hinder "the one" from coming to Christ. "The masses" sometimes keep "the individuals" or even the few from getting into the presence of His healing and saving power. Because of that, I am afraid there are many of those individuals who will never experience the joy and salvation that those of us who love Jesus have experienced.

While traveling down this road of evangelism, we need to ask ourselves some important questions. Are we, perhaps, an obstacle that prevents others from coming to the Divine Healer? Or are we an opportunity—perhaps the *only* opportunity—for those who are really sick to come into the Lord's presence? Are we a stumbling block or a stepping-stone? Do others have to stumble over us to reach Jesus—if they can reach Him at all? Or do we offer ourselves as stepping-stones on the path to Jesus?

I fear that, at times, we as Christians are so captivated with Jesus that we tend to "hog" Him for ourselves. We crowd around Him. We long to sit at His feet to learn more of Him and the love of God He brings us. And there is nothing wrong with that. But I am afraid that too often we do that at the risk of leaving no room for outsiders. I am afraid that we as Christians—and churches as a whole—can become so concerned with feeding ourselves on the Bread of life that we tend to forget about the hungry paralytics all around us who are starving to get a taste of the first crumbs of just *salvation* before they can even *begin* to enjoy the full loaf of *Bread* of a full and meaningful life in a daily walk with Christ.

When the "Christian crowd" gets in the way of lost individuals, then the healthy is hindering the sick. When we want so much of Jesus for ourselves that we make no room for others to get to Him, our evangelism is one-sided. It ceases to be the biblical method of evangelism which is so perfectly displayed in the life of Jesus, the Master Evangelist. Jesus Christ, as He is revealed in the Bible, is the norm for judging and shaping *all* evangelization. We will never encounter a greater or more useful idea in evangelism than that which is found in Jesus. He was, and is, and forever shall be the only *perfect* model evangelist.

There is nothing wrong with wanting to learn more about Jesus. There is nothing wrong with sitting at His feet to listen to His wonderful and inspiring teaching. There is nothing wrong with wanting to be in church every time the door is open because we are hungry for spiritual nourishment. There is nothing wrong with wanting to grow closer to Jesus. As a matter of fact, it is recommended. But when all we are interested in is feeding ourselves and growing more like Jesus, then I fear we are taking that desire to the extreme.

Yet, if the truth be known, if we sincerely *are* longing to be more like Jesus, then part of that longing will involve wanting to reach out to those paralytics of the world with the saving knowledge of Jesus. That desire to be more like Christ will motivate us to lead those paralytics to the only One who can heal them and cause them to walk again, and *nothing* will stand in our way.

In the movie, *Jurassic Park*, the actor, Jeff Goldblum, plays the character of a "chaotician." Apparently, it is a field which specializes in a philosophy similar to that of "Murphy's Law." If there is any way for something to happen, it will. In trying to explain away the impossibility of the regeneration of scientifically-created, modern-day dinosaurs, who were created without reproductive organs, he says, "Life will always find a way."

Remember when we discussed in an earlier chapter the importance of demonstrating love to those whom we are trying to evangelize? In evangelism, love will always find a way. And that is exactly what happened in this case of the paralyzed man. His friends loved him enough to go to any lengths to get him to Jesus, because they had enough faith to believe if they could just get their friend in the presence of the Master, he would be healed.

Love will bear almost any burden. Love will go to great lengths to introduce friends to Jesus. Love will even, sometimes, break the rules to accomplish its mission. Love does not give up easily. Love will not be too quickly discouraged.

We may, sometimes, be backed up by traffic jams on this evangelistic road, and we may not know what course of action to take. But if we care enough for the helpless paralytics of the world, creative and innovative methods in our evangelism will reveal themselves to us. We may not know exactly how to bring our lost friends to Jesus, but I assure you that love which is strong enough will always find a way. Perhaps it may not be so much the lack of proper methods as it is the lack of proper love, which prevents us from bringing our friends to Jesus. I have always believed that we should be twenty-first century Christians with a first-century message. There are times when we will need to change our methodology, but there will never come a time when we would need to change our message. So long as our methods are ethical, and do not contradict our theology, we do not need to worry too much about them. The same God who gave our spiritual ancestors appropriate evangelistic methods can be depended upon to give us the methods we need today.

The Bible teaches us over and over that we are saved by the grace of God through our faith which we put in His Son, Jesus Christ. But did you ever stop to think that our own faith in Christ's saving power, and our faithfulness can work miracles in the lives of our lost friends and family members? In Mark 2:5, we read, *"When Jesus saw their faith, he said to the paralytic, 'Son, your sins are forgiven.'"* Take note of what it says there. When He saw *their* faith.

All through the gospels we read how Jesus was amazed at the belief of certain Gentiles, and how He was equally amazed by the unbelief of His own people. Matthew 13:58 implies that Jesus could not do very many miraculous works in His own hometown of Nazareth due to the unbelief of the people. And we know that when they left Egypt, the Israelites wandered for forty years in the wilderness because they failed to believe the good report brought back to them by Caleb and Joshua.

It seems, therefore, that there is some sense in which our unbelief limits God, and some sense in which our faith liberates Him. How many of us owe our salvation, humanly speaking, to someone else's faith in the saving power of Jesus Christ? How many of us now believe in Him because some friend or family member first believed in Christ, and in us? So, in a very real sense, *their* faith brought us to Jesus Christ.

I know that if it had not been for the faithful prayers of my family, I probably would never have had my own spiritual awakening. Looking upon my own wretched lifestyle at the time, everyone knew there was no hope for this wayward preacher's son. But my parents never gave up. They believed God and claimed His promises, and rejoiced to see that their prayers were not in vain. There is a beautiful Christian song which has become very personal to me in which one line of the song says, *"You gave me love when nobody gave me a prayer."*

When nothing else has worked, and when everyone has given up hope, our own faith and faithfulness could be just the fulcrum needed to move a lost, paralytic out of the traffic jam of hopelessness and helplessness in his or her life to the other side of the bridge where they can, once again, freely move forward in the love and grace of Jesus Christ.

In the previous chapter, we metioned how there are some lost persons who live in doubt that Jesus could save someone as wretchedly sinful as they may be. They have made such a mess of their lives that there is no way that Christ can save them. But God's grace is limitless, His love is unceasing, and

His forgiveness knows no bounds. In Psalm 103:3-4, we read about the God *"who forgives all your sins, and heals all your diseases, who redeems your life from the pit and crowns you with love and compassion."* A few verses later David writes, *"He does not treat us as our sins deserve or repay us according to our iniquities. For as high as the heavens are above the earth, so great is his love for those who fear him; as far as the east is from the west, so far has he removed our transgressions from us"* (vss. 10-12). It does not matter how steeped in sin we may be, nor how hopeless our condition appears, there is always enough of God's grace and forgiveness to go around. That is the message of Good News we bring to all the paralytics who have no place to turn, who have become immobilized in their sin, and who cannot move forward until God's construction crew (we as Christians) opens the bridge to everlasting hope and peace and eternal life.

In John, chapter 4, we saw how Jesus was able to overcome physical, moral, cultural, and spiritual barriers to bring wholeness to a debauched, Samaritan woman. In John, chapter 5, we read how Jesus was able to meet the needs of a man who had been crippled for thirty-eight years. In John, chapter 9, we traveled the road with Jesus as He brought sight to a man who had been blind from the day he was born.

There is no case too hard for Jesus. He knew exactly what to do with this paralytic who required four men to carry him. He knows what to do with *all* persons. He can deal with what appears to be "hopeless" cases. We as evangelists and those to whom we are witnessing, need to know that Jesus can save, from the guttermost to the uttermost, all who come to Him in faith, believing. He accepts even those worst cases on which all the others have given up. He specializes in treating the world's rejects and outcasts.

As we read this incident in the life of Jesus, I sometimes wonder if we do not dwell long enough on the most important aspect of this healing. The physical healing of this paralytic appears to take front stage, and that seems to be what is all too often emphasized. However, Jesus deals with the whole person. The evangelism which pleases God is concerned with the whole person: body, mind, and soul.

When the paralytic was lowered to Jesus by his friends, Jesus said to the man, "Your sins are forgiven." The teachers who were also there were very disturbed by that statement and sat there, thinking to themselves, *"Why does this fellow talk like that? He's blaspheming! Who can forgive sins but God alone?"* (vs. 7). In Jewish theology even the Messiah could not forgive sins, and Jesus' forgiveness of sin was a claim to deity, which they considered to be blasphemous. But Jesus saw what this man needed most of all. He first met the man's deepest need: forgiveness.

Jesus, knowing what they were thinking, said to them, *"Which is easier: to say to the paralytic, 'Your sins are forgiven,' or to say, 'Get up, take your mat and walk?'"* (vs. 9). I have often felt that the point Jesus was probably trying to make was that neither forgiving sins nor healing was easier. Both are equally impossible to men, and, yet, equally easy to God.

At the heart of evangelism is the forgiveness of sin. As evangelists, we need to be crystal clear on that; and we need to make it just as clear to those whom we are trying to evangelize. I believe that in today's world we ceased "sinning" many years ago. In our "politically correct" society where we don't want to "offend" anyone, we have created a "no-fault" theology to deal with sin. People, even a lot of Christians, do not use the word "sin" anymore. They are no longer sins. They are "shortcomings," "failures," "mistakes," "blunders," "errors," or any number of other euphemisms.

If we want to remain true to biblical evangelism, using Jesus as our role model, we need to come to grips with the fact that evangelism deals candidly with the problem of guilt created by sin. Whatever else we as evangelists may do, if we do not deal with guilt over sin and help individuals find forgiveness for their sins, we are missing the mark. With all the "inoffensive" descriptions of sin we may use, and despite all of our own human "remedies" for sin, the problem of sin is still with us, and the only permanent answer to sin is forgiveness. *"The blood of Jesus His Son cleanses us from all sin"* (1 John 1:7, NASB).

Naturally, we want to be healthy, and we want our friends and families to be healthy. But the number one priority for us should be the spiritual health of those we love. We need to lovingly point out their sickness of sin, and then present to them the cure which only Jesus can give. We need to be careful not to fall into the trap of being part of the traffic jam that prevents the paralyzed who are stranded on life's sinful highway from bridging the gap between helpless desperation and glorious sanctification. We need to guard against the danger of being so eager to sit at the feet of Jesus to learn from His teachings, so hungry for Him to feed us, that we become part of the crowds—part of the "masses"—who block the way of those who are still lost in their sin, and who need His salvation.

This case of the paralytic is a miniature example of the church and the world today. The world is full of paralytics who need to be brought to Jesus. Some in the church are "hogging" Jesus for themselves so much that they comprise a crowd of Christians through whom there is no room for outsiders to pass. Others in the church are like the four men who are bringing paralytics to Jesus in spite of the crowds and all other obstacles. Still others are like the teachers sitting there, questioning in their hearts. They want to debate which should come first, the salvation of the soul or the "cleaning up of one's life" before they can embrace everlasting life.

As those who are trying to evangelize the lost, we need to work and hope and pray that when God heals that paralytic before our eyes, and when He forgives the sinner in our midst, we shall be amazed and praise God, saying, *"We have never seen anything like this!"* (vs. 12).

Against all apparent odds, these four men were determined to bring their sick friend to the only person who could help him. Just think how tragic it would have been if they had allowed the crowds to deter them from their mission. A paralyzed sinner would have been lost for all eternity, and the paralytic's friends and the rest of the people there would never have been able to see the wonders of God, and thereby spread the Good News of the hope and forgiveness Jesus offered.

One of the most moving and touching examples of not allowing the crowds to prevent one from accomplishing his intended purpose, was a testimony I heard a wheelchair-bound man share at a conference on Christian witnessing some years ago. The subject of this particular hour's discussion addressed the fact that we should never believe God is finished with us. As long as we are on this earth, He still has a work for us to do.

The man in the wheelchair was paralyzed from the waist down as a result of a bullet wound in his lower back which he had suffered when a burglar broke into his home one evening. During the break-in, besides permanently injuring the man, the intruder had also shot and killed the man's wife and nine-year-old daughter. The killer was never found and brought to justice. The incident became one of those cold cases which, unfortunately, far too many police districts have stuffed away in a box, gathering dust on some shelf in the precinct's basement. The trail had grown cold and there was nothing more that could be done to solve the double homicide.

For the next year and a half the paralyzed man sunk deeper and deeper into his own personal morass of despair, despondency, depression, and hopelessness. He began to drink heavily, curse his lot, and curse God. Finally, at the end of his rope one crisp, autumn afternoon, he decided the only way out was to take his own life.

He took a loaded gun out of his desk drawer, climbed into his specially handicap-equipped van, and drove down to a pier on the beach. Despite his own depression, he wanted his last sight of this world to be one of looking out over the ocean. It was a beautiful, sunshiny day with not a cloud in the sky. There were crowds of people moving everywhere.

The particular pier he had chosen had been a favorite of his wife's and daughter's, and they had spent many memorable, happy moments there. But the pier was so crowded with people, it would be difficult to maneuver his motorized wheelchair very easily between the people. So, he decided to go farther down the beach to another pier which was less crowded.

As he started to turn away, he happened to glance down at the far edge of the pier exactly where he had planned on ending his life, and noticed a little girl sitting there, and she appeared to be all alone. Memories of his own little girl stirred within his heart. He said he did not know why at the time, but for some reason he just felt drawn to this lonely-looking little girl. In spite of the masses of people, he started heading in the girl's direction. Many of the people he was trying to circumvent along the way grumbled their annoyance at him, but he just ignored them. When he reached the girl, he looked down at her and said, "Hey, honey, are you okay?"

She looked up at him with tear-filled eyes, and in a choking voice asked, "Please, mister, can you help me? I'm lost and I don't know how to get back home from here."

He asked what her name was and if she could tell him her address. She said her name was Elizabeth, and was, indeed, able to give him her address. He saw that she was shivering from the chilly wind coming across the water, and he gave her his jacket to wear, and told her he would be glad to drive her home, knowing her parents must be frantic with worry.

When they arrived at her house, she smiled sweetly, and thanked him as she hugged his neck. He watched as she opened the front door and stepped inside, and then he drove away, so touched by the encounter, that all thoughts of suicide had vanished from his mind. He had driven a couple of blocks down the street when he realized he had forgotten to get his jacket back from the little girl.

He turned around and drove back to her house, lowered himself out of his van, wheeled up to the front door and rang the doorbell. When a woman answered the door, he told her why he had come, and he was stunned by what the mother said to him.

She told him, "You're wrong, sir. How can you be so cruel to come to me this way? Our little Elizabeth was killed a year ago today by a random drive-by gang shooting. Today is her birthday, and she would have been nine years old today. She is buried out at the cemetery on the edge of town."

Completely at a loss for words, he just offered his sincerest and humblest apologies, and turned away.

He drove down to the cemetery, found the caretaker, and asked where the grave of Elizabeth was. When he found little Elizabeth's grave, he lost all control of himself and just hung his head in his hands and sobbed and sobbed for a good fifteen minutes. There draped over the tombstone marking Elizabeth's grave was his jacket he had given her to keep off the chill of the oceanic breeze.

When he left the graveyard, he went straight to the church his wife and daughter used to attend, and through tears of heartbreak he poured out his heart and soul in desperation and confession to the pastor. When he left the church that afternoon, he was a changed man, saved by the grace of God. He went on to become very actively involved in a local Christian ministry to handicapped people where he has been instrumental in reaching scores of persons who feel God has no use for "broken, useless" people.

He is quick to say that although we are tempted to underscore the apparent supernatural, angelic visitation from God to him at the end of that pier, the important thing to see here is, "What if I had allowed those crowds of people to prevent me from going down to the end of that pier? What if I had allowed their harsh grumblings to keep me from reaching out to a little girl who was lost and lonely? Regardless of how you want to explain that incident, the fact remains that if I had let such an 'inconvenience' hinder me, I wouldn't be here now, and a lot of one-time broken, discouraged lives would never have found true life in Jesus, the Savior."

My friends, there are countless numbers of paralytics all around us who are just waiting for a kind word and a helping hand from someone who cares. They are paralyzed by fear, doubt, insecurity, hopelessness, depression, discouragement, lack of love. They are paralytics who have become victims of their own feelings of emptiness and worthlessness, feelings of guilt and shame; persons who are desperately searching for direction for their lives, who are looking for a way to move forward, but they cannot do so because the bridge up ahead is out, and they have no place to go. They are stuck in the traffic jam of their sin, and they are either spinning their wheels or have been stopped dead in their tracks. They are waiting for someone who cares enough to reach out a hand and tell them, "Your sins are forgiven. Take up your mat and walk."

How about you? Have you been reaching out to any paralytics lately? Have you been concerned enough to use any method ethically possible? Have you had enough faith to believe God *can* save the hard cases? Was there a time when others thought you, yourself, were an impossible case? But then what happened? You received the touch of the Master's hand. You heard, "Your sins are forgiven." How did that make you feel? Do you remember? Wouldn't we want others to experience that same feeling? If so, then we need to reach out to those who are paralyzed by their sin and hopelessness and helplessness.

Let us not allow ourselves to be traffic jams along this road of evangelism preventing lost and dying paralytics from crossing the bridge from everlasting darkness to everlasting light.

CHAPTER 10

NO DEAD ENDS ON *THIS* ROAD

Wherever we drive across this great nation of ours, in villages, towns, cities, on country roads, neighborhood blocks, city streets, major highways, or even occasionally an interstate, we will inevitably come across the familiar sign which reads, "Dead End." At other times we will turn on to a street which will take us into a cul de sac back in a particular development. As we make the turn, there at the corner there may be a sign which reads, "No Outlet." Both of these signs warn us that if we continue in that same direction, we will eventually come to a place where the road just stops. There is no place else to go. Yes, we can turn around and go back the way we came, but that will not get us any closer to our destination. As we are driving around in unfamiliar areas, we can be grateful for these warning signs, which keep us from wasting our time by going down the wrong road. However, every once in a while we will find ourselves traveling down a street or road and all of a sudden there it is. A dead end. There was no sign to warn us this time. Now that can be really frustrating and even annoying.

In our lives today, we cannot help but run into some kind of dead end or another. A situation where there is no way out. One of those instances where we are brought to a complete stop, and there is virtually nothing we can do to remedy the problem. It could be financial, medical, economical, job-related. Dead ends just seem to abound sometimes in our lives. No matter what road we take, we always seem to eventually wind up at a dead end. At those times all we want to do is just throw up our hands and quit, cash in our chips, and simply say, "I'm done. No more. I can't take it any longer." And we all know that far too often some people really do throw in the towel, walk away from it, and end it all. I can think of very few tragedies so heartbreaking as that. Tragedies brought on by what appearsto be a totally hopeless situation. And in the mind of that individual that may very likely be the case. The person is facing such a severe crisis in his or her life which seems so bleak that it results tragically in one's own self-destruction. How desperate and helpless must a person feel to resort to such drastic measures? I cannot even begin to actually imagine such a thing, because I have never really been there. When I read of such incidents my heart goes out not only to the suicide victim, but also to the remaining victims left behind: the family and friends.

One thing that can be said about this road of evangelism, which cannot be said about any other road in life is that there are no dead ends. By that I mean there is no road in a person's life which dead ends at a place from which Jesus cannot rescue him or her. Of course, there will be walls and barriers and bumps in the road as we have discussed so far in this study. But no dead ends.

Please do not misunderstand what I am saying here. I am not adopting a rather flippant, insensitive attitude, ignoring the real pain and difficulties so many people face in their lives. I am not casually saying, "Well, just get saved, give it all to Jesus, and your problems will all go away, and it will always be 'pie-in-the-sky-by-and-by.'"

What I *am* saying is that the problems and the hurt and the heartache so many people feel are, indeed, very real. But they do not have to cause an individual to end up on a dead end street, and we as evangelists can offer to these individuals a way out, a way through their painful and, seemingly, impossible difficulties.

The apostle Paul tells us in Ephesians 2:1, that we are dead in our trespasses and sins. We know that God is alive. But because we are dead in our spirit and God is spirit, we are unable to communicate with Him. So, our spirits need to be made alive; and that's why Jesus came: to make us alive in Him, and thereby be able to commune with God.

As evangelists, we can be used by God to bring the dead back to life. Jesus is in the business of raising the dead. Jesus brings life out of death. Four times in the Gospels Jesus deals directly with death and restores life. In Mark 5:21-24, 35-43, Jesus brings to life the dead daughter of Jairus who had just died and was on her deathbed. In Luke 7:11-17, He interrupts a funeral which was already in progress to raise the son of the widow of Nain. The son was already in his coffin. In John 11:1-44, Jesus raises a man who had been dead for four days, and was already in the tomb! Finally, we know that Jesus dealt with His own death and resurrection. Let me repeat. Jesus is in the business of raising the dead. Evangelism is raising the dead. It is bringing life out of death.

I don't believe any study in evangelism would be complete without looking at the incident in John, chapter 11, about the raising of Jesus' friend, Lazarus. I have always felt this is one of the greatest miracles performed by

Jesus. I equate it on the same level of Jesus feeding over five thousand people with what was essentially a little boy's lunch. My finite mind just cannot grasp such incredible, unbelievable, and impossible scenarios. And if Jesus were not the One performing the miracles, they would, indeed, be impossible. But He is the powerful Son of God, and all things are possible with Him.

In looking at this incident of Lazarus, there is no question about whether the case relates to evangelism. Upon hearing about Lazarus' illness, Jesus told His disciples, *"This sickness will not end in death. No, it is for God's glory so that God's Son may be glorified through it"* (John 11:4). Then, later on in vs. 27, Martha confesses, *"Yes, Lord, I believe that you are the Christ, the Son of God, who was to come into the world."* And while standing by the tomb of Lazarus, Jesus prays *"for the benefit of the people standing here, that they may believe that you sent me"* (vs. 42). We further read in verse 45, *"Therefore, many of the Jews who had come to visit Mary, and had seen what Jesus did, put their faith in him."* Even the chief priests and Pharisees said about Jesus, *"If we let him go on like this, everyone will believe in him"* (vs. 48). There can be no doubt here that evangelism permeates every aspect of this incident in the ministry of Jesus.

Just as God created the world out of nothing, so through Jesus Christ He creates life where there is death. Paul tells us in 2 Corinthians 5:17, *"Therefore, if anyone is in Christ, he is a new creation; the old has gone, the new has come."* The similarities here are unmistakable. Evangelism is bringing order out of chaos. Evangelism is separating life from darkness, and causing the light to rule over that darkness. Evangelism is bringing life where there is death.

One of the things which made this miracle so amazingly significant to those present is that Lazarus had already been dead for four days! The Jews believed that after a person died, the soul would hover around the grave for three days, hoping for a reunion with the body. But at the first sign of decomposition—which generally started to occur on the fourth day—the soul would finally depart.

By what Jesus implied in verse 14, it is very possible, chronologically speaking, that Lazarus had died shortly after the messengers had left to go bring Jesus to the home. In verse 14, Jesus very plainly tells the disciples, *"Lazarus is dead."* When you allow for one day's travel from Bethany to Jerusalem, the two days Jesus remained after hearing the news, and then one more day for Jesus to make the trip to Bethany, Jesus knew His friend had already died.

An important evangelistic truth to be learned here is that death is not the end of existence. This is an important truth for both Christians and lost persons. As Christians, we can take comfort in knowing that there is a life beyond this life. Both Christians and non-Christians need to know that death cannot end their existence. That is one of the tragedies

which comes from suicide. Suicide victims are sadly mistaken if they feel that will end it all for them. There is no escape in this world or in the next. Even though Lazarus had been dead four days, this case teaches us that physical death is not the end of human beings.

What is probably the shortest verse in the Bible is found in this chapter where we read simply that *"Jesus wept"* (vs. 35). I believe this says to us that there is a place for tears in evangelism. Think about it for a moment. When was the last time you wept over the dead? I don't mean merely over those who have died in the Lord. Have you wept over those who have died without hope? I am sure all pastors share the same feelings when it comes to performing funerals for those who have died without Christ. The pastor feels helpless in that he cannot offer the family any real hope that there loved one is "better off," or that they will see their departed family member again.

Have you wept over those loved ones and friends who, although they are alive physically, are dead in their trespasses and sins? I am afraid that when we stop weeping, we may also stop winning. We need to ask God for the compassion and capacity to weep over sin which leads ultimately to the second death and to eternal separation from God.

I have no doubt that Jesus delighted in life's wholesome joys and pleasures, even though Scripture nowhere records His smiles or times of laughter. Yet He was so in touch with the heartbreaks of sin all around Him that He wept unashamedly at a tomb, shed tears over the unbelief of Jerusalem, and entered fully into the sorrows of sin-laden humanity.

Our Savior's tears encourage us to be true to our emotions, letting the Holy Spirit use them to overcome barriers and heal relationships. Moistened eyes often convey faith, honesty, caring, and love. Why cry? Because hurting, hardened, unbelieving people need Jesus, and they just might meet Him through our tears. If we have difficulty weeping over the lost, perhaps we need to ask God to open up our tear ducts.

As we mentioned earlier, one of the things which made this miracle so incredible was the fact that Lazarus had been dead for four days. It was hard enough for the people who witnessed this miracle to believe that Jesus did actually raise this dead man. But what made it even more difficult to grasp was that the man had been dead *four days*, meaning the body had begun to decompose and rot. Martha was appalled when Jesus told the people to take the stone away. So much so, that she commented in verse 39, *"Lord, by this time he stinketh: for he has been dead four days"* (KJV).

Jesus is in the business of raising the dead…those who are dead in their trespasses and sins. Even a soul which has begun to rot and decompose because of sin can be made whole and new again by the power of Jesus Christ, the strong Son of God. Does our evangelism allow for a Savior who can raise men from the dead even after they have been dead four days or longer? Some people appear to be more dead in their sins than others, even to the point that they are beginning to stink. Regardless of how wasted, rotten, and ruined a person has become, Jesus can restore new life to that person through His power and grace.

I recall reading about a woman in my home state of Kansas who remembered the grasshoppers of 1874. A lot of people are not aware of just how destructive these little insects really can be when they cover the earth in swarms. She related how these little critters stripped not only the crops but also the clothes from the settlers' backs. She stated, "They looked like a great white, glistening cloud, for their wings caught the sunshine on them and made them look like a cloud of white vapor."

We read in Joel 2:25, *"I will restore to you the years that the swarming locust has eaten"* (NKJV). Some of us, sad to say, have allowed the swarming locusts of this world to eat and devour so many precious years of our lives. They were years of waste and worry, years of emptiness, years of foolishness and pride, years of shame and slavery to the weak and destructive powers of this age. But the gospel we bring to others will restore those years which have been lost and stolen from dead souls who are not even aware that they *are* dead.

We hear so much about people all across the globe who are living in undeveloped and underdeveloped countries which are referred to as "The Third World." It was Peter Wagner who originated a term he called "the Fourth World" to describe the billions of people who make up the world of the lost. Can you somehow get a handle on that concept? As we sit and actually contemplate such a notion, the thought is just staggering. All across this planet there are billions and billions of people who are lost and dying in their sin, and as evangelists we are the only hope they have of ever hearing the Good News of how Jesus can bring life to their dead and decaying souls.

You may be tempted to say, "Well, I'm just one person and that number is just too vast for one person to attack." This is true. I don't argue that point. I don't really believe God expects us to save the entire world all by ourselves. And when you look at the big picture as a whole, it is, indeed, very discouraging. But as the saying goes, "Every journey begins with the first step."

Thom S. Rainer and Chuck Lawless have written an excellent book on church growth entitled, "Eating the Elephant." I would highly recommend the book to any church leaders interested in growing their church. In the book they address the idea of how one would go about eating such an enormous animal. In looking at the creature as a whole, it does look insurmountable. But they suggest attacking such an apparently impossible task the same way you would sit down to eat a nice, thick steak: one bite at a time. Although they are talking about growing a church in any given community, the same principle can be applied to reaching the billions of lost persons across this planet. No, we can never reach everyone. No, we can never save everyone. Even Jesus, Himself, said not everyone would be saved when He mentioned in the Sermon on the Mount that *many* would travel the broad road to destruction, and only a *few* would travel the narrow road to everlasting life (Matt. 7:13-14).

But even though we know we will never be able to spread the Good News to everyone, we can still approach that divine task one soul at a time. We have already mentioned that Jesus specialized in one-on-one evangelism.

There is one more truth in this incident I feel we need to address before moving on. That is the idea of eternal life. When people think of "eternal life," and when we discuss it with those to whom we are witnessing, the primary thought that is in their minds is that "eternal life" is something to be experienced "later." It is something "out there somewhere." It is something we will receive once we die.

But eternal life may be seen in this case as a present possession for those who believe in Jesus as their Savior. It is not just something hoped for in the future following physical death.

In John 11:21, Martha says to Jesus, *"Lord, if you had been here* [four days ago] *my brother would not have died."* To which Jesus responds by telling her, *"Your brother will rise again"* (vs. 23). Martha says in return, *"I know he will rise again in the resurrection at the last day"* (vs. 24).

You see, Martha's faith was in the Jesus of four days ago, and in the Jesus who would raise the dead in the resurrection of the last day. At that moment, she did not believe in the Jesus of today.

I am not saying this to be critical of Martha. Too often we are just like her. We believe more easily in the Jesus of the past and the Jesus of the future than we do in the Jesus of the here and now. Certainly, Jesus did mighty and wondrous deeds in the first century when He was here on this earth. Certainly, Jesus will work great and marvelous wonders when He returns to complete our salvation. But our faith needs to do some growing in the present. That same Jesus of the past and of the future is our Savior today. Hebrews 13:8 tells us that Jesus is the same yesterday, today, and forever. Eternal life is not pushed aside and placed on the back burner waiting for the consummation of the age after the second coming of Christ and death and the judgment. Right now and right here we are experiencing eternal life. That is the truth of eternal life in Jesus we need to impress upon those who may misunderstand the true meaning of this benefit of salvation. Eternal life is something we can experience *now*. It is something we can enjoy *now*.

Because Jesus has granted us eternal life, He has made us His children. And because He has made us His children, we know He will always be there to sustain us through some of the darkest hours we may face, even when we look death in the face. Even when we feel we have come to a dead end, we are not at the end of the road. There is always a way, and it does not mean we have to turn around and go back the way we came. Perhaps, like me, you have also heard it said that Jesus is a Bridge over troubled water. But I feel that does not say it accurately enough. I believe it would be closer to the turth to say that He is the Pilot *through* those troubled waters. We can rest assured that wherever Jesus leads us, whatever difficulties and trials and tribulations in which we find ourselves, whatever dead-end situations we face, whatever tumultuous storms rage around us, if we remain in the wake of Jesus, we have nothing to fear because wherever He takes us we know He has already been there and has already overcome it. Never doubt it, my friends. In the tragic storms of life, Almighty God specializes in calming waves and silencing winds. It will shock you at times. How can Jesus Christ save such a wretch as I? How can Jesus Christ do such a thing? How, indeed! He is God!

There is no such thing as eternal death, there is no such thing as a dead end where Jesus is concerned. No matter how hopeless and dead an individual is spiritually, that does not have to be the end of the road. Even if a person has been dead four days, we have a "fourth-day gospel" to share which restores life to the soul which has begun to rot and decompose because of sin. God is in the business of raising the dead.

God saved us Christians for a purpose. God uses men and women to bring others to salvation. Although it was *God* who raised dead Lazarus back to life, Jesus used others to remove the grave clothes in which he was bound. God wants to use us to remove the grave clothes of sin which bind so many hopelessly lost people all around us. Let's allow God to use us to take down the "dead end" signs marking the roads in the lives of lost individuals who are driving around aimlessly, looking for a way out of the cul de sac of their sin and confusion, wondering if they are ever going to find their way out. And just as importantly, let's allow God to use us to point those in the right direction who don't even know they *are* lost to begin with, and *won't* know until they do reach that one dead end from which there *is* no return.

CHAPTER 11

NO U-TURNS ALLOWED

We're driving down the street. We want to buy our car a new tank of gas; or we want to grab a bite to eat at a fast food joint; or we want to swing into a convenience store to grab a quick cup of coffee or some other item; or we want to pull into the post office to mail a letter or buy some stamps. We know our intended destination is at the intersection up ahead, and on the other side of the street. We've decided we'll just make a quick, little "U-ey" and pull right in. But when we get to the intersection, what do we see? Been there, done that, right? There in all of its annoying glory is that familiar rectangular sign that looks something like this: . Pretty frustrating, isn't it? Now we have to either keep going straight until we can turn around, or we have to turn at that intersection, go a little ways down the road, turn around and come back, so we can pull into the business's parking lot.

Oftentimes, our lives can be plagued by U-turns. There are those which are financial: just about the time when we think we are going to make ends meet, something always breaks in the middle, and we have to go back and start over again. Some U-turns can be job-related: we know we are in line for that raise or that promotion, but then the company folds, is downsizing, or we get passed over, and we have to start looking and hoping again. Then there are those U-turns which have to do with family: the family breaks up or a loved one dies, and we cannot seem to find direction for our lives, so instead of plowing forward, we just turn around and try to start reliving what used to be. And, of course, there are those proverbial medical U-turns: we are in the pink of health, but then all of a sudden we get slammed with a serious heart attack or a debilitating stroke, or we are laid flat with a terminal cancer, and our whole life comes to a standstill; and we now have to rethink our entire approach to life and all we had planned. Such U-turns can be absolutely devastating.

As we travel this road of evangelism, one truth we can impress upon people is that when it comes to salvation, we do not have to worry about

U-turns upsetting the apple cart. When Christ saves, it is for good—forever and always. There is no worry that something down the road will destroy our chance of being promoted from this life to a life of glory in heaven. There is no sin we can commit which will cause us to have to turn around and start all over again. There are some faiths and some people who will argue that point, using the example of murder and suicide as the basis of their argument. But as is always the case, when we are faced with difficult questions, we must turn to God's Word for the answers. In response to the above supposedly "exception" to our eternal security, I lift up for you I John 1:7: *"The blood of Jesus Christ, his Son cleanseth us from all sin"* (KJV). We read here that the blood Jesus shed for us on the cross, cleanses—purifies—us from *all* sin. It washes away *all* sin. Not all sin except murder or suicide, but *all* sin.

You may wonder why that would be relevant when witnessing to others about the salvation of their eternal souls. But, believe me, as a means to object to Christ's everlasting, saving power, someone may ask you that very question, and you will need to be able to give them an answer. Let's face it, folks, in this day and age people want to have absolute assurance about something before they take a step into unchartered territory in their lives. That is why it is so important for us to have a fairly good working knowledge of the Bible if we are to successfully witness to others. That's not to say we need to know the Bible by memory from cover to cover. But we do, at least, need to have a viably sound launching pad from which to venture into such a serious discussion about a person's lost estate and his or her need for what only Jesus can give them.

Two of my favorite Scripture passages on the Christian's assurance are found in John 10:27-29 and Romans 8:35-39. I encourage you to take a moment to read these passages to gain a better understanding of the eternal hope that is within us. I have included in the back of this book several Scripture passages which speak to this assurance we have in Jesus' salvation. I urge you to jot them down, place them inside your Bible or New Testament, underline or highlight the verses so you can quickly refer to them when needed. You never know when you may be asked the question, "Well, how can I be sure? How do I know for sure that I *will* go to heaven when I die? How do I know my loved one will be there waiting for me?" My friends, these are legitimate and valid questions, and we need to reassure others that, as Christians, they do have an eternal home in glory.

In Luke 23:32-45, we find an incident which, I feel, supports the truth that Jesus can save *anyone* regardless of who they are, how terrible they have been, or how "far gone" they may appear to be. This is Luke's familiar account of Jesus being crucified between two thieves who were deserving of their punishment.

We read in verse 39, that one of the criminals, his voice dripping with cynicism, *"hurled insults at him: 'Aren't you the Christ? Save yourself and us!'"* Jesus, being perfect and sinless, could have rebuked this man and replied just as cynically that who did this guy think he was? Jesus did not deserve to be there on the cross, but that thief certainly did, so who was he to talk? But that was not Jesus' way, and it certainly should not be our way either. Cynicism has no legitimate place in our evangelism. The cynic will be as ineffective as a door knob in evangelism.

The importance of confession in evangelism is seen in the other criminal's response to his cynical companion's remarks: *"Don't you fear God since you are under the same sentence? We are punished justly, for we are getting what we deserve. But this man has done nothing wrong"* (vss. 40-41). Before we can even begin to embrace salvation through Christ, we must first realize and admit our need and then confess our sins to God.

When you think about it, the bottom line is that there is only one thing really necessary for salvation, and that is turning from our sin and trusting in Christ alone to save. Baptism, church membership, prayer, and Bible study are all important if we want to be obedient to God in our Christian lives. But as important as all of those are, they are not the means by which we enter God's kingdom. None of these will gain an entrance into acceptance by God, or an entrance into heaven for all eternity. All our goodness, our good deeds, our charitable, loving actions fall far short of God's requirements for eternal life. Only by God's grace and by faith in Christ's shed blood can we ever hope to find forgiveness of our sins. It is only through confession of our sin that we can find hope for our hopeless lives. What kind of confession should we look for in evangelism? We should look for confession of *sin*.

I mentioned in an earlier chapter that we are not to read people a long list of rules of spirituality to live by on their way to salvation. We just present to them the Savior, and the issue of their relationship to Jesus. Hopefully, as they view their sinfulness against the backdrop of the purity and righteousness of the Son of God, they will see the hopelessness of their sinful condition and realize their need for cleansing through Jesus.

I worked for a while in a jewelry store, which was a rather educational experience all its own. One of the primary sales techniques we used was that when a customer wanted to look at a diamond, we would take it out of its display case and place it on one of the black felt pads scattered throughout the store. The idea, of course, behind that was that when the customer would see that bright, shining, lustrous stone lying on the dark, black background, it would enhance the beauty of the gem. That's how it is when we try to compare all our goodness and wonderful, unselfish deeds to the sinlessness and purity of the perfect Son of God. Seen in that light, we realize how far short we fall from measuring up to what God requires in order for us to be welcomed and embraced as one of His children.

This thief on the cross recognized his wretched, lost condition compared to the genuine goodness and perfection of Jesus, and realized he was hopelessly lost and bound for hell apart from what Jesus could offer him. He confessed what a sinner he was and turned to the only One who could give him hope, and simply said, *"Jesus, remember me when you come into your kingdom"* (vs. 42). How much simpler could it get than that? It is reminiscent of the parable Jesus told earlier in Luke 18:13, about the Pharisee and the tax collector who went into the temple to pray. The tax collector beat upon his chest and cried, *"God, have mercy on me, a sinner."*

Those to whom we witness, must be made to realize their hopelessly lost condition, confess their sin to God, and accept the sacrifice Jesus made on their behalf if they are to gain an entrance into the kingdom of God.

This repentant thief did not have a chance to be baptized, join a church, sing in a choir, tithe, or even read the Bible and pray. All that was left for him to do with the remainder of his life was to just simply die. He had no opportunity to do anything else.

According to this incident, we see that it is, indeed, possible for a person to be saved on his or her deathbed. So long as there is life, there is hope. Yes, this may be the only instance of a deathbed conversion in the Gospels, but it did happen, and it can happen again. So long as there is *physical* life, there is hope for *eternal* life. I am sure that I speak for a lot of pastors when I say we can certainly testify to such a thing happening in our ministries...and yet not only pastors, but lay Christians as well who have experienced such eleventh-hour transformations. I will elaborate upon that a little later in this chapter.

In response to the request from this dying thief, Jesus told him, *"I tell you the truth, today you will be with me in paradise"* (vs. 43). From this perspective, it appears that salvation is instantaneous in the ultimate analysis.

This case clearly establishes that it is never too late to come to Jesus. This is also a truth we need to impress upon those we are evangelizing. They may have waited a long time. They may have procrastinated time and time again. They might even feel that they have sinned away their day of grace. But this case shows us that now is not too late. It is seldom too late to get right with God. God's supply of grace knows no limits. God reminded Paul in 2 Corinthians 12:9, *"My grace is sufficient for you, for my power is made perfect in weakness."*

This thief was given the assurance that when he breathed his last on this his last day, he would be immediately in the presence of God. He did not have to be concerned that when he stood outside those pearly gates, his past, sinful life would be brought to bear upon whether he was qualified to pass through them. He did not have to worry that when someone looked upon his evil deeds, or that it was noticed he never lived a good Christian life or was baptized, or joined a church after his conversion, that he would be turned away at the last minute. He did not have to worry that he would be forced to make a U-turn, retrace his steps, and come back and try again when he was more "qualified" to join the ranks of those who had gone before him. Regardless of how brief his journey had been on this road of salvation, he need not fear coming face to face with a dead end—as we discussed in the previous chapter—and having to turn around and go back the way he had come. He had made his decision and that decision would serve him well throughout all eternity.

Another evangelistic truth we see here is the centrality of the cross. The cross is central to evangelism. Jesus' cross was in the center at the crucifixion. His cross is forever in the center of all crosses. All evangelism either begins at the cross or ends at the cross. It was Charles H. Spurgeon, the prince of preachers, who stated, "I take a text and then head straight toward the cross."

The cross is central in evangelism. It was certainly central in the life of the apostle Paul. He wrote in Galatians 6:14, *"May I never boast except in the cross of our Lord Jesus Christ, through which the world has been crucified to me, and I to the world."* The cross should be just as central in our lives and in our evangelism as it was in Paul's. We may boast in the cross because we are then boasting in what God had done for the salvation of the world.

If we are to get persons to come face to face with their sin, we need to bring them to Calvary, right to the foot of the cross. They need to come to grips with the fact that only through the cross will they find forgiveness for their sins; and only through death—the death of Jesus—will they find life...everlasting life.

We have all heard it said more than once that the ground is level at the foot of the cross, meaning, of course, that anyone and everyone is welcome there. No matter how rich or poor; famous or infamous; known or unknown; good or bad; powerful or powerless; all are welcome at Calvary. But by the same token, it is just as important to remember that the ground around the cross is anything but neutral. Neutral, we cannot be. Calvary requires persons to choose. God took His stand on that ground, and so must you and I, if we are to be faithful messengers of the cross. We need to bring lost people to the foot of the cross so they can decide on which side of the cross they will be taking their stand—the side of cynicism and insults, or the side of righteousness and everlasting life.

If they choose one side, their lives will be filled with continual U-turns, always turning around looking for another way to find direction for their lives, contentment for their souls, peace in their hearts, constantly feeding on the husks of the world, coming up empty and hungry and finding no nourishment anywhere.

If, on the other hand, they opt for the opposite side of the cross, they need never worry about losing their direction, having to make one U-turn after another, because what they are looking for is just as close as if it were right across the street, and yet try as they might, it is always just out of reach. They realize that once they begin their journey down this road of salvation, it continues to move forward, never backward, and they are never forced to backtrack and start the journey all over again.

Everything in the life and ministry of Jesus revolves around the cross. Think about it. The Cradle points forward to the Cross; and yet, without the Cross, the Cradle would have no significance. Even the Resurrection points back to the Cross. It *validates* the Cross. Our evangelism must also revolve around the cross.

We have mentioned before that evangelism was a passion with Jesus. He witnessed to a man even at the very end of His own life. Mark 1:14 states that Jesus came *"preaching the gospel of the kingdom of God"* (NKJV), and He died preaching that same Good News. Nothing, not even His own death, would keep Him from His Father's business.

What would happen, I wonder, if we allowed certain elements, obstacles, barriers, U-turns, to keep us from witnessing? Is it possible that we could lose our ability to evangelize by failing to evangelize when God gave us an opportunity? Our Lord was the perfect model evangelist, and He was presented with an opportunity to evangelize while He was nailed to a cross, and He seized that opportunity like He did all others.

I remember one of my favorite illustrations Dad would use in his sermons when I was growing up as a child; and I didn't know where that came from until years later when I had acquired my own copy of "Foxe's Book of Martyrs." I am sure almost every evangelistic-minded pastor has used this illustration at one time or another in his ministry.

Polycarp, one of the earliest Christian martyrs, was a student of the apostle John, and the overseer of the church in Smyrna. He was burned at the stake. He was told that if he denounced Christ, he would be released and would not have to suffer such an excruciatingly, painful death. Polycarp responded by saying, "Eighty-six years I have served him and he never once wronged me. How then shall I blaspheme my King who has saved me?" What a witness! The story goes on to say that when the dry sticks surrounding this saint were set afire, the flames rose up and circled his body without touching him. The executioner then pierced him with a sword and when he did, a great quanity of blood gushed out and extinguished the flames. Even though his Christian friends asked to bury the body as it was, the enemies of the Gospel insisted that Polycarp's body be burned in the fire, which was what was done.

Evangelism to the very end. Our calling as evangelists can *never* be laid aside. Jesus was witnessing even at the end of His own life. Those of us who have a calling from God can do no less. And you know what? We *all* have that same calling. None of us, as Christians, is exempt from the Great Command Jesus gave us before His ascension into heaven. *All* of us are called upon to be witnesses to the saving knowledge of Jesus Christ. We are *never* released from our calling to evangelize, not even in the face of our own deaths.

In chapter one, I made a passing reference to the spiritual legacy of a friend named Eddie. Yeah, I know what you're thinking: "*Finally*, he's gonna tell us." Well, that is, if you hadn't forgotten about it by now.

One Sunday at the conclusion of the services, I was approached by a dear, sweet, godly church member who was getting on in years. She told me how the family had just learned that her daughter-in-law's brother, named Eddie, had just been diagnosed with an aggressive form of cancer, and he was given no more than six months to live. He was not a Christian. As a matter of fact he was, and always had been, the farthest thing from being a Christian. She didn't know if it would do any good, but she asked if I would go visit Eddie and talk to him about his soul.

Not knowing exactly what approach I would use with someone like Eddie—a complete stranger—but after praying about it, I decided the direct approach would be best, just tell it like it is in so many words: "Eddie, you're dying. You've only got weeks or maybe months to live. You're not a Christian. Your life after this life is filled with uncertainty. But I'm here to help you with that, if you'll let me." I just felt that would be what would work best with Eddie.

When I drove out to his house that Monday afternoon, his sister was there with Eddie and the three of us sat around the kitchen table. He told me his sister had mentioned to him that I would probably be coming by for a visit that week, and he knew why I would be coming—that I wanted to talk to him about "gettin' saved." I asked him how he felt about that. He looked me straight in the eye, and as serious as he could be, he said, "Gene, I'm forty-six years old. I won't live to be forty-seven. I've wasted forty-three of those years, ever since I knew right from wrong. I don't want to leave this life the way I lived it. Tell me what I need to do...*please*. However long I have left to live, I don't want to live like that anymore."

I pulled out my New Testament, shared with him God's love, and explained to him the sacrifice Jesus made on his behalf, and what he needed to do to have peace and assurance not only for his few remaining months, but also when he would cross over to the other side. When I was finished he took ahold of his sister's hand with one of his own, and with his other hand he grasped mine and said, "Gene, that's what I want. Help me pray for it."

When we were finished praying, it was obvious a change had taken place in his life. He was a new child of God. There was such an expression of peace and calm and tranquility on his face, and through shameless tears he looked at me and just simply said, "Thank you, Gene, for telling me about Jesus."

Eddie lived for another five and a half months. He never darkened the door of the church. He was never baptized. He never became a church member. He was so sick from the cancer racing through his body that he couldn't leave the house except only to go back and forth to the doctor or the hospital, and even those trips were painful. But he never complained about his suffering. He was just glad to be alive and to experience the love of Jesus for his few short remaining weeks on this earth. Although he could not eat very much, he devoured his Bible. No matter how much pain he was suffering or how weak he was, he always had time for his Bible or for someone to read it to him.

That in itself would be a remarkable example of how Jesus changes lives, and how those who know Christ never have to worry about annoying, unpleasant U-turns which disrupt the flow of traffic on the road of salvation. But that is not the end of the story by a long stretch.

No one who came to visit Eddie, who had not heard it before, never left that house without first hearing Eddie's personal testimony of how Jesus had changed his life, and how He could change theirs as well.

During those five and a half months, through Eddie's witness, his other sister, his brother-in-law, two daughters, two brothers, three friends, one doctor, two hospice nurses, and his own mother came to know the Lord Jesus Christ as their Savior. They all went on to become very active, faithful members in their own respective churches, and witnesses for Christ in their own communities and places of business.

But the story doesn't stop there. As he lay dying on his bed at 2:30 in the morning, he looked around at the people surrounding his bed. His eyes came to rest on a hospice nurse whom he had not seen before. He asked her, "You're new here, aren't you? Are you a Christian? Do you know Jesus Christ as your savior? Do you know that you would go to heaven if you were to die tonight? If you don't, then you *can* know, just like I do."

He then looked at me and repeated the very first words that came out of his mouth after becoming a Christian: "Thank you, Gene, for telling me about Jesus."

He then looked up at the ceiling as if he were seeing something. He smiled, and a look of peace and great anticipation came over his face, and he said, "Yes, Jesus, I see you, and I'm a-comin' home." He then reached his hand up toward the ceiling...and then he died.

But the story doesn't stop there. After everything had been cleared away and cleaned up, that hospice nurse came over to me and said, "Please, pastor. I want to have that same peace that Eddie had. I want to know like he did that I'm going to go to heaven." She accepted Christ as her Savior before she left later that morning.

But it doesn't stop there. Two months later his last sister, Grace, came to my office one morning, distraught and weeping. She told me ever since Eddie had died, she had not had any peace. She was so troubled within her heart and soul. She wanted what Eddie had. She had loved her brother so much that she could not stand the thought of possibly never seeing him again. I shared with her the same scriptures I had shared with her brother. When she left my office forty-five minutes later, she was totally transformed. She knew one day she would see her brother again. Although she became active in the church after that, it did not last very long, because three weeks later she died suddenly and unexpectedly from a massive stroke.

And, yet, that is still not the end of Eddie's story. A year after Eddie had died, his final brother, Charles, landed in the hospital, also due to terminal cancer. When I went to visit him, tears came to his eyes when he saw me walk into the room. He grabbed my hand and squeezed it as tight as he could, and with a scared and trembling voice he said, "Pastor Gene, I don't want to die like this. I want to die like Eddie did. Please, *help* me."

Charles never left the hospital. Nine days later he joined Eddie and Grace in eternal glory. But during those nine days, Charles had led two nurses, one anesthesiologist, and one cleaning lady to the Lord.

As I reflect back on those moments, I am, as always, in awe of the saving power of Jesus Christ. And to think that it all started because one broken man did not want to see his life end the same way he had lived it, and was not ashamed nor afraid to share his testimony with others, and to let them know Jesus could do the same for them. What a legacy!

One time-honored and effective method of evangelism is the giving of your personal testimony. The skeptic may deny your doctrine or attack your church. The cynic may sneer at the message you proclaim, but he cannot honestly ignore the fact that your life has been changed. My friend, if you have not discovered the value of telling others how God has rearranged your life, you have missed a vital link in the chain of His blessing.

Death-bed conversions do happen. It is never too late for Jesus to save. No one is so lost in sin that the power of the cross cannot lift him or her up out of the deepest pits of their lostness. No one's life is so hopeless and steeped in sin that the grace of God cannot change that hopelessness into everlasting hope.

Before we leave this intersection on our road of evangelism, there is one last truth we need to explore. Perhaps, it is one that is all too often overlooked in our evangelism, one which we quickly skirt over.

In verse 44, we read that a curtain of darkness engulfed the earth. Could not that literal darkness be symbolical of the diabolical darkness of sin and evil which nailed Jesus to the cross? At the same time we read that the curtain of the Temple was torn in two. This was the curtain which separated the holy place from the holy of holies. Matthew's account of this same incident states that this fourteen-foot curtain was ripped in two from top to bottom, which means no human hands could have done that. This tearing of the curtain opened up the holy of holies to all people. Now *everyone* can come directly to God without having to go through some earthly priest.

No one will ever be able to put that curtain back into place again because of what Jesus did for us on the cross. However, another kind of curtain will fall on this world one day. Ever since time began, we have been moving from creation to judgment. God Himself will let down the curtain which ends history and consummates all things. We don't know when that will happen. We need to heed the words of Jesus in John 9:4 when He said, *"As long as it is day we must...work. Night is coming, when no one can work."*

In John 4:35, Jesus said, *"The fields are already ripe for harvest."* One of the things I learned working at the harvest time in Kansas, is that when the wheat turns white, it is already overripe. It begins to fall out of the husks and away from the stalk. We do not know how much longer God will give us to reap and to sow. Because of that, we need to work all the more diligently before that last curtain falls and we will not be able to work anymore in this age.

All around us there are lost persons who are "merrily" driving down the various roads in their own lives, as "happy" as can be, seemingly without a care in the world. All is well. They are at peace with the world, with others, and with themselves. Their lives seem to be marked with contentment and satisfaction. They know where they are headed in life.

Then all of a sudden they reach an unfamiliar intersection of their lives. They can clearly see where they want to go, where they need to be to accomplish their goal, and it may constitute having to turn around and go back the way they came. But they cannot do so because there's that annoying sign. They are stopped dead in the middle of the intersection. They can't go forward. They can't turn left or right. They can't go back. Because by going in either of those directions, they will miss their intended destination. They are at a loss as to what to do or where to go. They have no place to go to find lasting peace and satisfaction.

Thank God, that when we start out on the road of salvation, we never have to worry about running into U-turns which prevent us from reaching our ultimate destination in Jesus. Nor do we need to fear that when we have finally reached the end of life's road, that someone or something will shove a sign in front of us telling us we need to go back because we still have not met all the requirements.

That is the hope of peace and assurance we have to offer to those around us who have wasted so many years of their lives and may not even know it. But the question comes to us. Are we on the lookout for those opportunities God places within our reach to evangelize those who need to find a way through that intersection of snarling traffic which burdens them down and continually beats them into the pavement?

Evangelism is anywhere we want to find it. Jesus found it on a cruel cross. Polycarp found it on a fiery stake. Eddie found it around a kitchen table. Charles found it in a hospital bed. Where will you and I find it?

CHAPTER 12

ROAD UNDER CONSTRUCTION

---

*I*mprovements along our nation's roadways are a constant necessity. Yes, they can be a real nuisance at times, but if we want to continue to enjoy smooth, unhindered driving across our country, there is no way to avoid such inconveniences. In most instances the nature of the construction is such that we are able to drive around it. At other times, the construction is so serious that the road ahead is blocked completely and is impassable, causing us to have to take a detour around the work site. Regardless of the type of construction going on, the need for such improvements is almost always a result of weather conditions, outdated road structures or traffic patterns, the constant, daily traffic of thousands of vehicles, or it could be just plain old age…the pavement has just worn out and it needs a new shot of concrete-and-tar adrenaline.

Just as the roads across our nation are constantly being worked on, so are our lives once Jesus takes control. Paul writes in Philippians 1:6, *"The one who began a good work in you will continue to complete it until the day of Christ Jesus"* (NAB). Paul is telling us that when we become Christians the God who began this wondrous work of salvation in us, will keep on working in us until Jesus returns to take all of us Christians to be at home with Him. From the moment we accept Christ as our Savior, God is constantly working, molding, fashioning, shaping, building, and constructing us to conform to the image of His Son.

Sometimes the road construction He is performing within us may not be too pleasant. As a matter of fact, it may be downright painful. But as in any construction, there needs to be some tearing down before there can be some building up. Paul writes in Galatians 2:20, *"I have been crucified with Christ and I no longer live, but Christ lives in me. The life I live in the body, I live by faith in the Son of God who loved me and gave himself for me."*

Paul is talking about being crucified with Christ. When Christ was crucified, what happened? He died. Elsewhere, Paul talks about having died with Christ (Romans 6:8). Any way you want to cut it, being crucified is painful. Dying is painful. So, if God needs to do some tearing down in our lives in order to do some road repairs, we need to expect a little pain and discomfort along the way.

But prior to the road work needed in our lives after becoming Christians, God has to do some preliminary work to prepare us for that. That means He has to break through that hardened, old pavement surrounding our old selves, so He can begin the new work of bringing us to a saving knowledge of His Son, Jesus Christ, thereby creating a *new* self.

The gospel of Luke is the Gospel to the outcasts. In Luke 19:1-10, we read about an outcast who needed some major road work done in his life. This is the familiar story concerning a little guy we all learned and sung about in Sunday school. His name was Zacchaeus. Zacchaeus was a despised tax collector. But not just any run-of-the-mill tax collector. He was a *chief* tax collector, which made him all the more hated, despised, and corrupt; and this also made him that much more of an outcast. He may also have been an outcast because he was a *"short man."* He apparently was also very rich; and his wealth was probably acquired by unscrupulous means.

Yet, despite Zacchaeus' bad reputation, Jesus did not scorn him as the rest of the townspeople did. Jesus loved him rather than judged him. It is a striking parallel to the incident we read about in John 8:1-11, where a woman caught in the very act of adultery was brought before Jesus, and He was asked by the woman's accusers what should be done to her. Jesus did not condemn nor judge that woman. He just loved her the same way he just simply loves each and everyone of us, no matter what our sin or what our past or present life may have been.

When Zacchaeus heard that Jesus was coming to town, he ran ahead so he could get a better look at this man everyone had been talking about. He was curious to find out what all the hoopla was about regarding this man called Jesus. We know the story how Zacchaeus climbed up into a sycamore tree to get a glimpse of Jesus as He passed by.

As He was walking by, Jesus looked up and saw Zacchaeus. Jesus notices those who notice Him. Jesus was especially aware of outcasts. He still takes note of them today. If we want to pattern our evangelism after that of Jesus, we must also take notice of the outcasts. Even though they may not necessarily be outcasts from society, they may be feeling outcast deep within themselves, feeling they have no purpose in life, feeling they have no hope of ever being any better off than they are right now. If we are crucified with Christ to the point that He is seen living in and through us, perhaps some lost person's curiosity will get the best of him or her, and they will ask us for an answer to the hope that is within us. Would we be alert to such an opportunity if God ever presented it to us?

There may be persons around us who are small of stature, not physically, but emotionally and spiritually. As evangelists, we need to make them aware that Jesus loves them. Jesus is aware of them. Jesus sees them. Jesus will not overlook them. Jesus never missed anyone who wanted to see Him.

Jesus took the initiative with Zacchaeus. He told him, *"Zacchaeus, come down immediately. I must stay at your house today"* (vs. 5). We should learn how to take the initiative with the lost. We should meet them more than halfway. We should be willing to go that extra mile. At the very least, we should be willing to meet them on their own turf. Jesus did.

Jesus said in verse 10, *"The Son of Man came to seek and to save what was lost."* Our God is the God who seeks.

If we are going to find those who are lost, we need to get out from behind our desks. We need to leave the comfort of our homes and churches. We need to put feet to our prayers. The time is long past when the majority of the lost will themselves come into our churches. The time is long past when the majority of the lost will themselves approach *us* seeking answers to their questions, and seeking solutions to their problem of sin. The truth of the matter is that a great many lost people do not even know they have a problem called sin, and that they need that problem solved. They do not realize the pavement on the roads in their lives is damaged and useless and in need of repair. We are the ones who need to go looking for *them*.

If we are to pattern our evangelism after Jesus, we have to take the initiative with the Zacchaeuses who are up the sycamore trees of our world. Those sycamore trees whose foliage is the sin that has taken root in the lives of lost men and women everywhere, and whose limbs are shaky, weak, and rotting, and about to break, dropping these lost souls into the bottomless pit far below them.

Zacchaeus' life was in shambles. He was a thief, a crook, a cheat, a self-centered man who was probably only interested in how much he could swindle out of the town's citizens and how much of that he would be able to keep for himself. If anyone needed major road construction in his life, it was Zacchaeus.

Because Jesus took time to notice this outcast, we can see the dramatic and profound change in Zacchaeus. In verse 8 he says to Jesus, *"Look, Lord! Here and now I give half of my possessions to the poor, and if I have cheated anybody out of anything, I will pay back four times the amount."*

There should be some evidences of changes in the lives of our converts. There ought to be obvious signs that some major road construction has been performed in their lives.

The apostle Paul writes in 2 Corinthians 5:17, *"If anyone is in Christ, he is a new creation; the old has gone, the new has come!"* Those who have embraced Christ as their Savior ought to give evidence that their lives have undergone major road construction.

The gospel of Mark is often considered a fast-paced Gospel. We read quite frequently such phrases as "immediately," "at once," "quickly," "just then." But did you ever stop to think how this witnessing experience for Jesus seems to move along rapidly? Right from the outset, we get the impression that Jesus was in a hurry. We read that He was just "passing through" Jericho (vs. 1). Zacchaeus "ran ahead" (vs. 4). Jesus said to Zacchaeus, *"Come down immediately"* (vs. 5). Zacchaeus "came down at once" (vs. 6).

Jesus appeared to be in a hurry, but not in so much of a hurry that He could not take time to spend with someone who needed His salvation.

When you examine the evangelistic ministry of Jesus, you see that a lot of His witnessing was done while He was "passing through" on His way to some other destination to help somebody else. When we feel rushed and in a hurry, we would do well to follow Jesus' example. We should never be in such a big hurry that we do not have time to share the Good News of Jesus with those who need to hear it. We need to keep in mind that *all* road construction takes time to accomplish its intended purpose.

Jesus was a master at impromptu evangelism. He was prepared for that unexpected opportunity. Whenever one presented itself, He reached out and seized it. He may have been passing by, or passing through, but He never passed up an opportunity. What about us? Are we prepared to do that kind of evangelism? Do we know how to latch on to those spontaneous possibilities?

In discussing the definition of evangelism in the opening pages of this book, we mentioned converting "persons and structures to the Lordship of Jesus Christ."

You will recall that "structures" was used to identify the family structure, and how we read in the Bible that entire families were brought into the Kingdom of God. Just as in the case of Cornelius (Acts 10:1-11:18) and the Philippian jailer (Acts 16:22-34), we see another instance here. When Jesus says in verse 9, *"Today salvation has come to this house,"* it is implied that the entire household may have also found the salvation that Zacchaeus did.

Let's face it, folks. When the head of a household finds salvation, it cannot help but affect the entire family. And it does not necessarily have to be the head of the household. It could be another family member.

While it is a real joy to see the head of a household saved, it is an even greater joy to see how the salvation of that one individual can affect his or her family and friends. God can use that one individual's salvation as a bridge over which He can cross to reach other lost persons on the other side.

Even though I was just a child at the time, I remember a stirring event which took place at the conclusion of a worship service shortly after Dad became pastor of the church we could see from crest of "The Hill" which I mentioned in an earlier chapter.

As the invitation was being given, down the aisle walked a father and his two sons. The wife was already a fine Christian woman. Within a matter of just a couple of minutes another husband and wife and their two sons also walked the aisle on the other side of the church. Both families, who were close, were our neighbors up on "The Hill." As a matter of fact, both of their pairs of sons were the exact same age as my sister and I, so we, obviously, hung out a lot together. Needless to say, Dad was overjoyed to see these two families come to know Christ as their Savior. I can still see that look on his face that morning. Both families became very close friends of our family and they were all very active in the church.

I have always believed that the wonderful Christ-like example of that sweet, Christian wife and mother was probably the catalyst that prompted her husband and two sons to make their decision for Christ; and very possibly was the encouragement the other family of four needed to make that same decision.

As exciting as it is to see an individual come to know Jesus as Savior, it is even more exciting to hear our Master say, "Today salvation has come to this *house*."

When I think about such conversion experiences as those, and the one about Eddie which I shared in the previous chapter, is it any wonder that evangelism can, indeed, be exciting, just as my evangelism professor, Dr. Miles, used to say? As much as we appreciate, and are grateful, for being saved, it is certainly more fun, and provides more peace of mind and heart when we see our loved ones and friends saved along with us.

Through God's grace and by the saving power of the shed blood of Jesus, God begins a new and good work in each of us when we confess

Christ as our Savior; and He continues to carry that work on to completion until the day Jesus returns to take us home to be with Him, or until we pass from this life into the next.

There are lost persons all around us—wherever we want to find them—whose internal roads are cracked, broken, filled with pot holes, crumbling and falling apart. They are in a serious state of disrepair. They have been worn down by the daily traffic of sin that continually traverses across their hearts and lives. The inclement weather of this world's storms have repeatedly hammered and chipped away at the foundation which has held them together for so long, but now it is being mercilessly torn out from under them. Only the divine construction crew of God and His Son, Jesus Christ, can perform the much needed repairs; and only you and I, through our witnessing, can prepare the pavement ahead of time for the divine machinery to do its work.

At the time I was writing this chapter, I had recently attended the interment services of a dear, dear Christian friend of mine. He was one of the finest Christian men I had ever had the joy and privilege of knowing. He loved the Lord with all his heart. He loved working for the Lord in God's house and throughout the community. He never hesitated to speak a word about the goodness of God.

One of the traits I always loved and admired about him was his genuine concern for lost persons, and his excitement when one more soul was added to God's kingdom. He could never seem to do enough for the One who had given him eternal life. He could never tell others enough about the love of Jesus. He had said more than once that God is always doing something new and great and wonderful in his life. He would remark, "God just keeps on working and working. You'd think that after a while He would take a break and start in on somebody else, but that's just not His style. But I don't mind. I know I will be a better person because of it." He was faithful to the end, and was always looking for one more way to serve his God just simply out of gratitude for what God had done for him.. His favorite song was Andre Crouch's great hymn of praise, "My Tribute."

> "How can I say thanks for the things you have done for me?
> Things so undeserved, yet you give to prove your love for me.
> The voices of a million angels could not express my gratitude.
> All that I am, or ever hope to be, oh, God, I owe it all to thee.
> To **God** be the glory."

God had finally completed the work in him which He had started. How significant, I thought, that he was buried in a section entitled, "The Garden of the Evangelist." As I stood by his grave, with tears running down my face, I was reminded of Paul's final words to his son in the ministry, Timothy, which happened to be the very words my friend was hoping could some day be said about him: *"The time has come for my departure. I have fought the good fight, I have finished the race, I have kept the faith. Now there is in store for me the crown of righteousness, which the Lord, the righteous judge, will award to me on that day--and not only to me, but also to all who have longed for his appearing"* (2 Timothy 4:6-8).

May that be said about all of us as evangelists, and about all those whom we evangelize. God wants to do a great work. Are we willing to let Him use us to help Him begin and finish that great work He wants to perform?

CHAPTER 13

SHORTCUTS CAN BE COSTLY

---

*I*t has always been our human nature to try to get from one point to another as quickly as possible, especially if we are traveling down a road, whether that be riding or walking, unless, of course, we are just on a nice, leisurely, relaxing drive or hike through the countryside. This desire to want to get to our intended destination as quickly as possible has certainly increased over the years as we have moved into the fast-paced society in which we now live. Because of that, we can be grateful for those shortcuts we sometimes find along the way, which speed up our progress. We have to admit that they do save time, of which we are very appreciative.

My oldest son and his family currently live on the lower Eastern Shore of Delaware, what is referred to as "slower, lower Delaware." He has lived there virtually all his life, and he knows that area like the back of his hand.

I used to know the area fairly well myself, but having been away for so long, I've lost most of my bearings down there. He and I have jokingly remarked more than once, how he can drive me ten minutes away from his house, taking all kinds of back roads, shortcuts, and what appears sometimes to be nothing more than wilderness trails, and he has gotten me as lost as a blind man wandering through a maze. But he knows exactly where he is at any given moment. And if by some chance *he* ever gets lost down there, his sense of direction is so sharp and acute, that within minutes of driving around, he will know exactly where he is and how to get back to where he wants to go. He has familiarized himself so much with that area that he knows all the shortcuts and the quickest way to get from one place to another, whether he is going into town, going to work, going to church, or going to the beach.

As helpful as shortcuts can be, all of us know that the important thing to remember about them is that if they are to be of any use to us, they must be the *right* shortcuts. And, guys, I don't want to be accused of "taking sides" here, but it seems that husbands are the most notorious for saying, "I know a shortcut," and then end up taking the long way around. But we all know that if we take a wrong shortcut, it will very likely turn into a "long cut," and we could very easily become lost, turned around, and possibly even be in danger. At the time we took those shortcuts, it was the way we wanted to go. Even though we may have thought it was also the way we *needed* to go to save time, it turned out that was not the case at all. Sometimes what we want is not always what we need.

We can all remember at Christmastime making a list of what we wanted to see under the tree on Christmas morning. Sometimes we got our wish, and sometimes we didn't. But in all fairness, we have to admit that even though we may not have always gotten what we wanted, what we did get oftentimes turned out to be exactly what we needed. We may have wanted a particular type of bicycle, or pair of jeans, or pair of shoes, or doll, or some other toy, like all the other kids would probably be getting. But when we opened the present, it turned out to be something similar, but not quite the same. Even though we were glad to receive it, we could not help but be a little disappointed because it was not exactly what we wanted. But let's be honest, my friends, experience has taught us that sometimes the least expensive brand lasted longer than that name brand "all the other kids" had received. When theirs had bitten the dust, ours would keep going…

and going...and going, like that Eveready bunny. It turned out to be what we wanted after all.

In evangelism, those to whom we witness must be made aware that shortcuts can be costly. We must help lost persons realize that what is wanted may not be what is needed, and the price paid for taking that shortcut can be the price of their eternal souls.

In Acts, chapter 3, I see an example of want versus need, and how the want could have been disastrous if *that* had been met instead of the need. This incident occurred in the ministry of Peter and John during the infancy of the Church. This is the scene where Peter and John were going to the temple and a crippled beggar asked them for money, but the apostles healed his broken body instead. Although the miracle takes place in just the first ten verses, the entire chapter should be read to understand the full meaning of what has happened here, especially as it relates to evangelism.

Everyday someone would bring this beggar to the temple gate called Beautiful so he could sit there and beg for money from those going into the temple. It was his way of surviving from day to day. I am sure, from a business standpoint, this must have been an ideal location for the beggar to set up shop. How could people, with any kind of normal conscience, going in an out of the temple to worship God, refuse to give a handout to a beggar at the temple gate? Besides, it was considered an act of obedience to God to give to such beggars in need.

We have all heard the expression, "Give a man a fish, and he will eat for a day. Teach that same man *how* to fish, and he will eat for a lifetime." That same principle, I feel, can be applied to this incident.

Verse 2 states that this man had been *"crippled from birth."* He had been unable to work for a living his entire life. He had to beg daily for just enough to get by. Through no fault of his own, he was looking for a "quick fix." He was looking for a shortcut to simply get by from day to day just as he had done all his life. This was the only life he knew. He knew nothing else. He knew of no other way to "make it." So, when Peter and John came walking by he was expecting a few more coins to be handed to him. This is what he wanted, but not what he needed. As a matter of fact, he really was unaware he *needed* anything else.

This man had become so accustomed to living the way he had all his life, that he truly felt there could never be any other lifestyle for him. Every single day, the same mundane routine. He's taken to the temple. He sits and begs all day long. At the end of the day he's taken back home to survive on what little he may have acquired that day. He was resigned to the fact that this is how he was going to live out his existence. Day after day…week after week…month after month…year after year. Can you even imagine that kind of hopelessness? I certainly can't. And, yet, that is what this man's life consisted of. There was never any hope that things would ever change for him.

It is very possible that this man also had become embittered by his lot in life. All his life he had never been able to walk or run, dance or jump, or even work for a living the way he had seen so many others all around him do. How often must this pitiful man have said to himself, "If only I could do that, too. But not a chance. Here I am in this broken-down, useless body, not good for anything. How I wish I could do all those things as well." His wishing would turn into longing, and his longing into deep-seated bitterness, even to the point that he may have become quite cynical in his attitude. We don't know that's what happened. But human nature being what it is, and sheer hopelessness being as emotionally and mentally destructive as it is, it is quite possible this cripple had developed that kind of mindset.

Then along comes these two men going to the temple to worship, and as was his custom, the man asked them for money. Take a moment to examine this scene. It is very likely this sullen, broken man was not even paying attention to Peter and John when they walked by. He was just going through the motions of begging as he had done for years, probably voicing that same mantra he had used over and over, "Alms for the poor. Alms for the poor," or something similar. The verses seem to bear that out. Verse 3 says, *"he asked them for money."* Then in verse 4 we read that Peter said to him, *"Look at us!"* This man had not even been paying them any attention. Probably from the corner of his eye, he just saw two live bodies walking toward him, and he went into his spiel.

At Peter's command, the cripple gave them his undivided attention. Peter then tells the man, *"Silver and gold I do not have, but what I have I give you. In the name of Jesus Christ of Nazareth, walk"* (vs. 6). What Peter is essentially telling this man is that, "We don't have any money to give you, and, quite frankly, money is not what you really need, even though it may be what you want. You need something far more valuable than money, and that's what we are going to give you." We read in verses 7-8 that Peter took this man by the hand and *"he helped him up, and instantly the man's feet and ankles became strong. He jumped to his feet and began to walk."*

I see three very significant truths in this miracle as it relates to evangelism...truths that perhaps are sometimes overlooked because we are concentrating on the actual miracle itself.

The first truth I see here is that Peter said to this man, *"In the name of Jesus Christ of Nazareth, walk."* Peter wanted to make sure there was no doubt in anyone's mind who was going to be responsible for this healing.

When we hear the name, "Jesus," today, we immediately think of the Jesus of the Bible. But we have to remember that "Jesus" was not an uncommon name back then. "Jesus" is the Greek form of the Hebrew name, "Joshua," both of which mean "savior." So, when parents named their son "Jesus" or "Joshua," they did not do so lightly. They were attaching a great deal of significance to that name, unlike today when parents oftentimes give certain names to their children because they just simply like the name.

Peter wanted the observers of this miracle to know this was not just "any ol' Jesus" he was talking about. Peter identified this Jesus as "Jesus Christ," which is significant. The term, "Christ" means "Messiah." So, in case anyone questioned who this Jesus was, they would know right away that Peter was talking about Jesus, the long-awaited Messiah, who had caused such a stir over the last three years, and had just recently made the headlines because of his trial and crucifixion. Yet, Peter went one step further in identifying who he was naming, when he said it was "Jesus Christ of Nazareth." This firmly nailed down who was going to receive the credit and the glory for this miracle. It was common knowledge that this Jesus who proclaimed Himself as the Messiah was that Nazarene from Nazareth.

In evangelism, it is most important that we stress to others there is no one else—and nothing else—who can save a person's eternal soul. There are no shortcuts on the way to heaven. We cannot take a shortcut around the cross. We cannot avoid expressing faith in the Son of God—the God who saves us by His grace through the shed blood of Jesus. Jesus said, *"I am the way and the truth and the life. No one comes to the Father except through me"* (John 14:6). The writer to the Hebrews says, *"Without the shedding of blood there is no forgiveness"* (Hebrews 9:22). Paul writes in Ephesians 2:8-9, *"It is by grace you have been saved, through faith—and this not from yourselves, it is the gift of God—not by works, so that no one can boast."*

Yes, these verses are all too familiar to us, but those to whom we are witnessing need to realize they cannot avoid this crucial step in their salvation. They cannot take a shortcut to everlasting life by doing great works and wonderful deeds. And when you think about it, it seems that would actually be the *long* way around, because when would you know you have done enough good works to warrant a place in heaven, and how would you know that some mistake or sin would not cancel out all those good deeds you had done? You would be lost all over again, and you would have to go back the way you had come and start the journey again, as we mentioned when we were discussing "dead ends" and "U-turns."

Yes, doing wonderful deeds, performing good works, treating your fellow human beings with respect, dignity, caring, understanding, and even love may be what lost persons *want* in order to earn an entrance into heaven, but it certainly is not what they *need*. They need *"Jesus Christ of Nazareth."*

The second truth I see here is that this man believed the message of Peter. He placed his faith in someone he did not even know. Granted, he may have heard about Jesus. He may have even seen him a time or two. After all, he had been crippled all his life, and he had been brought to this temple gate for years, and we know Jesus had gone into the temple Himself on more than one occasion. So, it is very possible this crippled man had, indeed, seen Jesus.

What I find so significant about this man's faith is that he did as he was told without question or argument. When you think about it, that in itself was quite an achievement for this broken man. He didn't know who Peter and

John were. He probably had no idea who this Jesus was except what he had possibly heard through the rumor mill. And, yet, he exercised complete faith in these strangers and their message.

He could very likely have cynically argued and even ridiculed Peter and John. He could very easily have laughed and scoffed at them and said, "What?! You kiddin' me? What kind of trash are you talkin'? C'mon, now. Get real, fellas. You *must* be jokin'! Look at me! I've been this way all my life, and there ain't no way I'm ever gonna get better. Go sell your nonsense somewhere else. Cantcha see I'm workin' here?" He *could* have said that, but he didn't. As a matter of fact, he didn't say anything. He just took Peter's extended hand and stood up. He did not understand how this was going to happen. He did not question the possibility of something "impossible." He did not say, "Well, let me think about this for a moment." He just exercised his faith in something he did not understand and his whole life was changed from that moment on. He would never be the same again. He would never have to have someone carry him to the temple gate again. Never again would he have to sit and beg for something to eat. Now he could go out and learn a trade and earn his own way in life. He was no longer dependent upon a fish a day to eat. He had been "taught how to fish," and now by his own ability he could fish and eat the rest of his life. What he wanted was money to live one more day and continue to take the usual shortcuts to survival. But Peter gave this man what he needed so he could find his own way.

There seems to be no question here that this man was saved. We read, *"He jumped to his feet and began to walk. Then he went with them into the temple courts, walking and jumping, and praising God"* (vs. 8). He was not thanking Peter and John. He was not admiring his new-found ability to move around the same as everyone else he used to envy. He was *"praising God."* This one-time cripple knew to whom he should give the thanks and glory for the miracle wrought in his life. He knew that it was the power of God through Jesus Christ of Nazareth, which now made it possible for him to walk.

In our evangelistic efforts, we need to help persons realize that even though they do not understand how salvation becomes real in their lives simply by exercising their faith in the Son of God, it does happen. This is one of those areas in life which we cannot really explain to the inexperienced. One of those realities which just has to be experienced in order to believe and appreciate it. All the explanations we can think of can never fully satisfy the curious of heart and mind. It is all of faith, and even that faith does not originate within us. It comes from God. We ask God, "Lord, help my unbelief.

Give me faith to believe in you." And He does. When we are sincere, God will always give us what we need, even the faith necessary to believe in His Son for salvation, even though we may not know anything about Him.

The third truth I see here is that this man's healing was immediate. Verse 7 says that *"instantly the man's feet and ankles became strong."* I see here not only God's healing power, but also his divine grace and strength. The crippled man did not have to test his legs to see if they were strong enough to hold his weight. Immediately, his muscles received the strength necessary. He had been crippled all his life, but he did not have to *learn* how to walk, how to put one foot in front of the other, how to shift his weight from one leg to the other, how to hold himself erect. By God's grace he immediately knew *how* to walk, and even jump.

When God saves, He saves instantaneously. He does not ask us to do a lot of "other things" before our salvation is complete. We do not have to go from house to house, knocking on doors, inviting others to join our cause in order to assure us a place in heaven with Jesus. We do not have to add a lot of good deeds to our lives to prevent us from losing our salvation. We do not have to continually confess our sins to another individual—another sinner—in order to grant us access to God. Paul writes in 1 Timothy 2:5,

"There is one mediator between God and men, the man Christ Jesus." Our salvation happens instantly. There is no waiting around. There is no wishing and hoping and wondering if we truly are going to make it to heaven. Just as this man knew immediately how to walk, so we can know immediately that we are saved children of God, and we, too, can jump and praise Him.

Three truths we need to impress upon those we are evangelizing. Only Jesus Christ can save their eternal souls. Only by exercising faith, and faith alone, in Him will they ever receive that salvation, not by anything they have done or will do, but only by faith in Christ. When they receive Him as Savior, their salvation is immediate. They do not have to wait until they die before they really know the truth of that. Through God's grace and the power of Jesus, they are able to know right away and for the rest of their lives.

Just as Jesus before him—and later Paul—took advantage of every opportunity to evangelize, likewise Peter did the same here. In verse 16, Peter tells the onlookers, *"By faith in the name of Jesus, this man whom you see and know was made strong. It is in Jesus' name and the faith that comes through him that has given this complete* [including spiritual?] *healing to him, as you can all see."* Peter goes on to say in verse 19, *"Repent, then, and turn to God. So that your sins may be wiped out."* Peter was given the opportunity to share the Good News with these people, and he seized it.

In the preceding verses Peter reminded these naysayers that Christ had come to seek and to save those who were lost, but He was not what they wanted. They wanted someone or something else, so they killed the only hope of salvation they had, the one Person they needed for acceptance by God. Yet, God in His grace, raised Jesus from the dead, giving them another chance to go by way of the cross, and not take that shortcut which looked much more appealing.

Remember when we mentioned in an earlier chapter, that skeptics may deny our doctrine or attack our church; or cynics may sneer at our message, but they cannot honestly ignore the fact that our lives have been changed? Peter uses that same approach here to convince these people that Jesus is the One responsible for this miraculous healing. In verse 16, Peter refers to this former cripple as *"this man whom you see and know."* And he refers to his healing *"as you can all see."*

Peter had made a point to emphasize the fact that it was Jesus who had brought healing to this man. This was a man whom they had all seen for years begging at the temple gate, and they all knew his story. Now, here is that same man walking around and jumping as if he had been doing it all his life. Peter is telling these "astonished" observers that whether they understand it or not, whether they want to believe it or not, here is proof!

One final aspect of this incident, I feel, bears mentioning. We read in verse 7 that Peter took this man by the hand and helped him up. Peter did not allow this cripple to try to accomplish something he had never done before on his own. This was something brand new to this man, maybe even a little scary. This was new territory and he needed help, and Peter was there to give him the help he needed.

My friends, when we witness to others to embrace, by faith, the Son of God so they can have eternal life, for some of them we are essentially asking them to turn their backs on everything they have ever known or believed throughout their entire lives. And *that* can sometimes be scary. We are asking them to deny a lot of what they have been taught by parents, trusted friends or family members, or, sad to say, even some church pastors. They need help to understand that some of the shortcuts in their lives that they have been used to taking, will only lead them to eternal separation from God. No, it will not always be easy, and we certainly will not win everyone to whom we witness. But that must not prevent us from doing what we can to help them see the correct road to travel. And those who do embrace our message, will give us cause for rejoicing as we see them jumping and praising God.

There are those all around us who are wanting a quick fix, a shortcut around the cross, depending upon themselves and their own abilities to gain acceptance by God. They do not realize that what they want is not what they need. Sadly enough, far too many are not even aware they are on the wrong road, that they have taken a shortcut which will cost them their eternal souls. That is why it is so important, as evangelists, for us to lovingly extend a hand to them to help them up out of their helpless, crippled condition, and, as scary as it may first appear, to help them overcome their apprehension, so they can walk in a newness of life.

CHAPTER 14

THE IMPORTANCE OF THE HIDDEN ENTRANCE

We are driving down a street in any given community, or maybe a back road out in the country. Up ahead on the right we see one of those yellow caution signs which reads "Hidden Entrance." The referenced road is an entrance into a little neighborhood tucked back into a housing development, or it is a road which leads back toward a person's property or house. The sign is there because that particular road may be set back away from the main road and there are so many trees or so much shrubbery lining both sides of the entrance that not knowing it was there, and driving by, it would be virtually invisible. We know the sign is there to warn us to be on the lookout for vehicles emerging from that entrance, in order to prevent possible accidents. If the sign were not there, it is very possible we would never know that road even existed.

The hidden entrance serves a very important function. It provides egress and ingress to and from a particular destination. Without it, there would be no access to an individual's home or, perhaps, place of business. It is very necessary, and all hidden entrances have only one way in and one way out.

Did you ever stop to think that there are "hidden entrances" on this road of evangelism? Well, there certainly are, and they play a very important and crucial role in evangelizing the lost. They are, indeed, "out there" and we may know about a few of them, but the vast majority of them are completely unknown, and, yet, we can thank God for them. Without them Christianity would never have become what it is today, nor would Christianity be able to move forward as it continually does year after year. As we study the ministry of Jesus and observe the beginnings of the Chruch in the book of Acts, we see them over and over.

I am referring to all the unsung heroes of evangelism down through the centuries who have plodded along year after year spreading the Good News to lost people everywhere, and never receiving the well-deserved attention for their ceaseless and tireless efforts. Don't misunderstand what I am saying here. I am not stating that when we see lost persons come to know Jesus Christ as Savior under our witnessing, that we should be applauded for the work that we do. That certainly is not the reason we should be sharing the gospel with those who need it. If that *were* the reason, then it ceases to be true, biblical evangelism as demonstrated by Jesus, and we become no better than the scribes and Pharisees with whom Jesus was always locking horns. I will elaborate upon this point in more depth at the end of this chapter.

In Acts 8:26-39, we see one of those unsung heroes. This is the familiar story of Philip witnessing to the Ethiopian eunuch. This is a perfect example of doing God's will and following the leading of His Spirit even though we do not have a clue as to why He wants us to do a particular thing or perform a particular task. To understand the full impact of that truth it is really necessary to read verses 4-8 of this chapter.

We see here that Philip went down to a city in Samaria. When the people heard the message of Jesus that Philip proclaimed, a great revival broke out in that city. So great was it, that we read in verse 14, *"When the apostles in Jerusalem heard that Samaria had accepted the word of God, they sent Peter and John to them."* I guess you might say they brought in "the big guns" to follow up on the evangelism of Philip and to help nurture and grow these new Christians in their faith.

Then in verse 26, we read that out of nowhere, *"An angel of the Lord said to Philip, 'Go south to the road—the desert road—that goes down from Jerusalem to Gaza.'"*

Just like that. Philip is not even told why he should go. He is just told to go. He is not even told what he is to do once he gets there nor whom he is supposed to see…if *anyone*. Here Philip is in the midst of a great spiritual awakening, proclaiming the Good News of Jesus to perhaps hundreds of people and seeing scores of individuals embracing Jesus as their Savior, and all of a sudden God tells Philip to just "up and leave."

That's how it is sometimes when we serve God. He has plans for us that we know nothing about. Yet in His wisdom and omniscience He always knows exactly what He is doing. It is not for us to try to figure Him out. We are just to follow His lead, believing He will always lead us exactly where He wants us to be at any given time in our lives, and He will always be there with us to sustain us, guide us, and give us His grace. Paul writes in Romans 11:34, as he quotes Isaiah, *"Who has known the mind of the Lord?"* It is not our place to question God, and Philip did not do that either. He just left, as he was instructed to do.

We do not know how long Philip had been traveling down this road, but eventually he learned the reason why God wanted him there.

Philip came upon a *"very important official in charge of all the treasury of Candace, queen of the Ethiopians"* (vs.27), sitting in his chariot reading from the book of Isaiah. This was a very significant and well-trusted VIP in the kingdom of Ethiopia. You might say he was the Secretary of the Treasury of the entire nation of Ethiopia. He was responsible for how all the moneys were distributed and brought into his country. These types of positions were not handed out lightly. The queen had to have had a great deal of respect and admiration for this nameless man, and believed deeply in his unvarnished integrity.

We read that Philip approached the man and heard what he was reading, and simply asked him if he understood what it was he was reading. To which the eunuch replied, *"How can I unless someone explains it to me?"* (vs. 31). Verse 35 tells us, *"Then Philip began with that very passage of Scripture and told him the good news about Jesus."* What Philip did two thousand years ago is no different from what we are called upon to do today: Simply tell the Good News about Jesus.

We are told that after Philip explained salvation to the eunuch, the man believed in Jesus as his Savior and was baptized, and *"When they came up out of the water, the Spirit of the Lord suddenly took Philip away, and the eunuch did not see him again, but went on his way rejoicing"* (vs. 39). Just like that. Suddenly Philip was there, and then suddenly he was gone.

We do not know how much time Philip spent with this Ethiopian eunuch. It may have been a few minutes, or it may have been several hours. What we do know is that God wanted Philip to leave in the midst of a great revival so he could witness to *just…one…man.* The incredible spiritual awakening which was taking place in that unknown city of Samaria was very important to God. But just as importantly, was the need for Philip to leave in the middle of it, so he could share the Good News with only a single individual, even if it comprised only thirty minutes of Philip's time.

As you have read this, you may be thinking that, yes, Philip was one of those unsung heroes, and you would not be entirely wrong. However, he is not the "hidden entrance" I am talking about. I am talking about that unknown, nameless Ethiopian eunuch. We never see nor hear from this eunuch again, and yet we read he went on his way rejoicing.

This was a very influential man in his country who had the ear of the queen herself, and important dignitaries not only in his own country of Ethiopia, but very possibly in other nations as well. When he spoke, people listened. It is not hard, then, to see why God wanted Philip to leave his great evangelistic meeting to go witness to this one individual.

In following the leading of God's Holy Spirit, Philip was helping to fulfill the command given by Jesus to His disciples in Acts 1:8, when He told them, *"You will be my witnesses in Jerusalem, and in all Judea and Samaria, and to the ends of the earth."*

In returning to Ethiopia with the Good News of Jesus Christ in his heart, this eunuch was now helping to extend Christianity beyond the borders of its birthplace. No, we do not know this man's name, but we do know that he became a hidden entrance for others to travel that road to salvation. If it had not been for him, how many souls, I wonder, would never have known about Jesus? No, he did not receive the praise and accolades from his peers, but he did receive that pronouncement from Jesus when he crossed over into glory: "Well done, good and faithful servant."

As we examine the life and ministry of Jesus, we see many such unsung heroes—those hidden entrances, nameless, unknown individuals who, having been touched by the healing and saving power of Jesus, spread the Good News about Him.

Matthew 9:27-31, tells us that after Jesus had restored sight to two blind men, they went out and spread the news about it all over that region.

In Mark 1:40-45, we read how, after Jesus had healed a man with leprosy, the man went out and began to talk freely, and spreading the news.

In Mark 5:1-20, after Jesus had cast out the demons of a man in the region of the Gerasenes, the man went and told people how much Jesus had done for him.

We are told in Mark 7:31-37, that when Jesus had healed a deaf and dumb mute, neither the healed man nor the people could stop talking about it.

These are just a very few examples of people touched by the saving power of Jesus, and how they witnessed to others about what Jesus had done for them. I cannot help but believe that as a result of their testimonies, many more came to know Jesus as well.

We also read that on more than one occasion the people healed by Jesus went their way praising God and giving Him the glory. They were not going to take credit for any of this. They knew who was responsible for their transformation, and they wanted others to know about it as well.

Whether we are talking about the miracles in the Bible, miracles which happen in our lives today, or the salvation of a lost person's soul (which has to be the greatest miracle of all), God is the One who receives all the glory. As evangelists, we do what we do for the glory of God and not for the praise of men; and those who willingly receive our message will also give God the glory.

One of my best friends E-mailed me a video which very clearly addresses this subject. The video is entitled, "The Invisible Woman." A lady by the name of Nicole Johnson, who is affiliated with an organization called, "Freshbrewed Life," is addressing a large audience of what appears to be mostly women.

She is sharing with the group how she had been feeling like an invisible woman. She would walk into a room, tell the family to turn the TV down, but she would be ignored, and she had to do it herself. At a party, her husband didn't seem to acknowledge her even when she came up to stand by his side. When her son was asked by his teacher who she was, the son just replied, "Nobody." Obviously, she began to feel very down about all of this and was feeling like an invisible woman whom no one seemed to see or acknowledge.

One night she was with a group of other ladies who were celebrating the return of a friend from England. Mrs. Johnson had put her makeup on in the car, she was wearing an old dress, with her hair just pulled back in a banana clip. She was feeling pretty pathetic.

While sitting around the table, the returning friend gave Nicole a book on the great cathedrals of Europe. Naturally, she did not understand until she read what her friend had written inside the front of the book: "With admiration for the greatness of what *you* are building when no one sees."

She went on to explain to the audience, "You can't name the names of the people who built the great cathedrals. Over and over again, looking at these mammoth works, you scan down to find the names, and it says, 'Builder unknown…unknown…unknown.' They completed things, not knowing that anyone would notice. There's a story about one of the builders who was carving a tiny bird inside a beam that would be covered over by a roof. And someone came up to him and said, 'Why are you spending so much time on something that no one will ever see?' And it's reported that the builder replied, 'Because *God* sees.' "They trusted that God saw…*everything*. They gave their whole lives for a work—a mammoth work—they would never see finished. They showed up day after day. Some of these cathedrals took over a hundred years to build. That was more than one working man's lifetime. Day after day. And they made personal sacrifices for…no…credit. Showing up at a job they would never finish, for a building their name would never be on. One writer even goes so far to say, 'No great cathedrals will ever be built again because so few people are willing to sacrifice to that degree.'"

She continued, "I closed the book and it was as if I heard God say, 'I see you. You are not invisible to me. No sacrifice is too small for me to notice. I see every cupcake baked, every sequin sewn on, and I smile over everyone. I see every tear of disappointment when things don't go the way you want them to go. But remember, you are building a great cathedral. It will not be finished in your lifetime, and, sadly, you will never get to live there. But if you build it well, *I* will.'

Mrs. Johnson concluded by saying, "It's okay that they don't see. It's okay that they don't know. We don't work for them. We work for *Him*. We sacrifice for *Him*. Let's pray that our work will stand as a monument to an even greater God."

It's easy for us to think of some of the great names of great Christians and evangelists throughout the history of the Christian Church. We are reminded of Paul and Peter and John, Martin Luther, John and Charles Wesley. Men like D.L. Moody, Charles Spurgeon, Billy Sunday, J. Wilbur Chapman, R.G. Lee, L.R. Scarborough. Men in our own time who have had great ministries such as Charles Stanley, D. James Kennedy, Charles Swindoll, W.A.

EVANGELISM: A Road Less Traveled

Criswell, and Billy Graham, who have made great inroads into Christianity, church growth, and evangelism. These men have been responsible for great strides in evangelism, and seeing many souls come to know Christ as Savior under their ministries, because they love the Lord, and they have a burning desire to see lost people come to salvation, not for their own glory, but for the glory of Almighty God.

But, my friends, if it had not been for the millions and millions of those "hidden entrances"—those unsung heroes—who poured out their hearts and lives into the cause of Christ because they, too, have loved the Lord, and have had an equally burning desire to see lost people come to salvation—not for their own glory, but for the glory of Almighty God—Christianity would *never* have become the mighty, unstoppable force that it has. And I know that everyone of those well-known Christian servants mentioned above, and so many others like them, would whole-heartedly agree, and stand up and say, "Amen!"

I have not written this chapter to mislead anyone into believing that I feel, as evangelists, we should receive, at least, *some* credit for the work that we do for Jesus Christ. As I mentioned earlier, that is not why we do what we do. I really had no intention of writing such a chapter as this. However, I feel the Lord has just impressed upon me to write these words as an encouragement to all those unsung heroes and hidden entrances who may sometimes get discouraged as they work and work in the Lord's harvest fields, trying to provide a way for lost and dying souls to find their way home, and they feel they are spinning their wheels on this road of evangelism, not seeing any visible results.

You may be a struggling pastor in a small church, faithfully witnessing week after week from the pulpit and from house to house, and you feel God must be through with you because there does not appear to be any change. Or you may be the pastor of a *large* church which seems to have come to an impasse, and you see no visible growth. You may be a church staff person or lay Christian leader trying to share the gospel with a Sunday school class, home Bible study, family member, friend, or co-worker, and you are feeling what appears to be the futility of your efforts.

If you happen to be one of those who are struggling with such feelings, let me just say that you *are* only human, and God understands. He feels your pain, your hurt, your disappointment, and your heartache. He does, indeed, see every tear of disappointment you cry. Everytime you share His love with someone else, it does not go unnoticed. He does hear every prayer for strength and grace and for the lost that you utter. To all of you unsung heroes let me remind you of God's promise to us through His apostle, Paul.

"Let us not become weary in doing good, for at the proper time we will reap a harvest if we do not give up" (Galatians 6:9). *"Therefore, my dear brothers, stand firm. Let nothing move you. Always give yourselves fully to the work of the Lord, because you know that your labor in the Lord is not in vain"* (2 Corinthians 15:58).

One of the most moving illustrations of how God strengthens and encourages His servants when they become discouraged, is one my father oftentimes would use. Even now, years later, it still moves me and touches me deeply. He related the story of a missionary who was returning home after devoting the greater part of his life to the mission field in Africa.

The old missionary was returning home to the United States after spending almost fifty years on the Dark Continent. His body was broken, withered, and emaciated from so many difficult years in the mission field fighting malnutrition, diseases, physical injury, and heartbreak. He had suffered time and again from the devastating effects of that harsh African climate. His leathery skin was wrinkled and in some places appeared to be just hanging on his bones. He had lost much of his hearing and his eyesight was very poor. He walked with a very noticeable limp and needed the help of a cane to move around. He had lost all of his family and a lot of his friends to either the elements or unfriendly natives. He could barely speak above a whisper. He was physically broken, as well as heartbroken, without a family, and all alone. During his fifty years in the mission field, he had been able to only make three trips back home to America.

Returning to America on the same ship as this faithful old missionary, was President Theodore Roosevelt. The President was returning from one of his many famous safari trips he would often make to that continent. The hunt had been extremely successful, for the President had several new trophies to add to his collection.

Thousands of people had gathered at the harbor in New York to welcome their President home as he walked down the ramp from the ship. Bands were playing, groups were singing, people were shouting and waving, banners were flying, flags were billowing. Through the downtown area where thousands of more people lined both sides of the streets, a huge ticker tape parade, escorted by squads of New York's finest, accompanied the President to his lavish quarters in New York City's grandest hotel.

When the ship had docked at the harbor, down another far distant ramp, all alone, walked this wrinkled old missionary hobbling along with the help of his handmade cane. No bands were playing. No flags were waving. No one was singing. No parade to welcome him home. There was no one to escort him through those semi-dark streets to his small, dimly-lit, one-room, windowless hotel accomodation, which had just one small bed, one table, one chair, and a leaky, cracked sink in the bleak bathroom. He shuffled through those streets all alone, stoop-shouldered, head bowed, and hands shaking.

When the missionary laid his battered, little old suitcase on the table, he fell to his knees by the side of the bed, and poured his heart out to the God he had served so faithfully all those years.

He prayed, "Dear God, you know I have never been one to complain, and I have always enjoyed serving you as faithfully as I could all these years. And I'm not complaining now. I'm just asking you to help me understand how a man who has spent a few weeks hunting and killing animals can receive such a tremendous welcome home; and a poor broken-down missionary who has sacrificed so much, and has lost so much, and has poured his whole life into telling others about the love of Jesus, has no one at all to welcome him home."

That tired, old, worn-out missionary would later write in his little diary that it seemed at that very moment a wonderful sense of peace and the presence of God enveloped him, and he felt God speak to his heart, "Missionary... you're not home yet."

My dear friend, you may be a hidden entrance, a nameless, unsung hero. You may never have your name engraved on a bronze plaque or chiseled on a stone monument. But let me assure you, *God* knows your name. *He* knows who you are, and the work that you do. Let us all be thankful to God for those "hidden entrances," those unsung heroes, on this road of evangelism who have helped pave the way for the advancement of the Kingdom of God, and who have helped provide an entrance for God's children into His—and their—heavenly home. Perhaps you, yourself, may have been one who found his or her way home because of a hidden entrance.

CHAPTER 15

EVANGEILSM: A ROAD THAT NEVER ENDS

As soon as a driver turns onto Route 50 off of Coastal Highway (Route 1) in Ocean City, Maryland, located right on the Atlantic Ocean, he immediately sees a green, overhead sign with white lettering which states: "Sacramento, California 3073 miles." If it were possible to stretch Route 50 out into one continuous, straight line, eliminating all the twists and turns, hills and valleys, rivers and streams, cities and mountains between Ocean City and Sacramento, you would see before you a long, never-ending ribbon of black-top as far as the eye could see. Just as you can stand on the seashore and gaze out across the vastness of the ocean, and be tempted to say it is endless, so you could stare down that long, transcontinental highway and think that it, too, has no end. But we all know that eventually the ocean does come to rest at another far, distant seashore somewhere; and we know that, over 3000 miles in the distance, Route 50 would also ultimately cease to be a road any longer. Route 50's horizon would eventually become its dead end.

We have been traveling down this road of evangelism for some time now, encountering various kinds of bumps, dead ends, U-turns, and other obstacles. Some of them have been similar in nature, and some have been quite different. But the one constant about this road we have been traveling, is that *this* road *never* ends. There is never a place along this road where we will finally come to an end and we can stop. The only ending for this road will be when God calls us home to be with Him, or when Jesus returns to claim us for His own. Jesus, Himself, said in John 9:4, *"As long as it is day, we must do the work of him who sent me. Night is coming, when no one can work."* There are three important truths which immediately jump out at me from this statement of Jesus.

The first truth I see here is that Jesus tells His disciples, "*We* must do the work." Not Jesus only, but Jesus and His disciples. This command of His is communicated over to us as well, which brings me to the second truth in His statement.

The second truth here is that Jesus tells them, "We must do the work of him who sent me." God sent Jesus into the world to minister, and to evangelize.

This is the same task which Jesus gave to His disciple—and to us—upon His ascension into heaven. God sent Jesus, and now Jesus has sent us.

The third truth, and the one we will be discussing in this chapter, is that Jesus warned that "Night is coming when no one can work." I feel we can safely assume here that Jesus is talking about evangelization. God sent Him into this world to bring Good News of great joy to all people. That was His work. Jesus is telling us that, as Christians, we are all called to do this same work.

Christ is saying we are to continue to witness whenever we have the opportunity, and as long as those opportunities present themselves to us. We are never relieved of our duty to evangelize the lost. As long as there is breath in us, we are to continue to spread the Good News of Jesus. Our road of evangelism never ends.

The book of Acts is an exhilarating book about fascinating people, dramatic events and great truths. But did you ever stop to think that it is the only "unfinished" book of the Bible, practically speaking? I say that because we are still "writing" the history of the Church day by day. How exciting to be a part of what God continues to do in and through His Church. The task of the universal Church of Jesus Christ is incorporated into the *local* church. While the depth of any church is determined by the quality of its worship and instruction, the breadth of any church is determined by its commitment to fellowship and evangelism. We must keep reaching out to people who are in need. After all, that is what love is all about.

We do not all have the same gifts, talents, and abilities. All of us do not start on this road at the same time. Some start early in their Christian life, some start midway, and others don't really take up that task until later on in their lives. As we mentioned earlier in this study, whether we see any visible results from our labors or not, we are still to be faithful witnesses of our Savior, Jesus Christ. And regardless of how many, or how few, gifts God may have given us, or where in our Christian lives we start down this road, our Master will reward us according to His grace and in His own time. One of the most beautiful and touching illustrations of this is one I will share at the end of this chapter.

In Matthew 20:1-16, we read the familiar parable by Jesus about the laborers in the vineyard. We know how the story unfolds. A landowner goes out at different times of the day and hires several people to work in his vineyard. A few he even hires during the last hour—the eleventh hour—of the day, and he promises all of them he will pay them whatever is right. At the end of the day, the owner paid each of the workers the same amount of money, which was equivalent to one day's wages.

Those who were hired at the first hour of the day, began to grumble and complain because those who were hired at the end of the day were paid the same amount as those who had toiled all day long in the heat of the day, and had to bear the burden of most of the work. The owner answered them by saying, *"I am not being unfair to you. Didn't you agree to work for a denarius? Take your pay and go. I want to give the man who was hired last the same as I gave you. Don't I have the right to do what I want with my own money? Or are you envious because I am generous?"* (vss. 13-15).

This parable promises us that if we start even at the eleventh hour, we shall receive more than we ever hoped. Even though we start at a fearful disadvantage, we may still be made equal with those who started at sunrise. The parable also seems to imply the fact that often those repenting late may overtake those who started long before they did. It is not the length of service that tells the faithfulness of a worker, but the quality of that service.

In this parable Jesus reveals the basis on which rewards will be distributed to those who have committed themselves to Him. People may waste precious hours of the day when they could be serving their Lord. But our Lord never sits idle. He is always moving about, looking for those who are willing to work diligently in His vineyard. At various hours of life's day, we can begin to work for Him. As He demands the longest day of service we can render, He promises us wages—or rewards—based upon our diligence.

The kind of mood demonstrated by the grumblers mars discipleship with discontent. The Landowner, being just, knows what each laborer of His is worth. Therefore, discontent at His rewards for service is unwarranted. All who enter His service must enter with the full persuasion that their labor for Him will not be in vain. As His laborers, we are guaranteed a full and just remuneration for our service, whether it is long or brief. Each of us will receive the due recompense of the reward. God will never be unfair to us. We will never be cheated by God.

God has called us to be workers in His vineyard—the world around us. We have been sent by Him to evangelize the lost. God really did not give us any choice in the matter. Jesus said, "You *will* be my witnesses." He did not ask us to think about it for a while. He did not ask us to try to squeeze it into our busy schedules. He very clearly commanded, "You *will* be my witnesses."

As Christians, God is our Lord and Master. He is within His rights to grant us particular gifts and talents as it has pleased Him. He has every right to place us in the Body of Christ where He pleases. He has every right to reward us as He sees fit according to our faithfulness.

God never treats us unfairly nor unjustly. Nor does He reward us unjustly. If we are faithful and diligent in our service to Him, if we serve Him cheerfully without complaining, He will reward us accordingly...if not in this life, then certainly in the life to come. And it matters not if the lost person to whom we are witnessing becomes a Christian at that time or later on down the road through the witness of someone else, or doesn't become a Christian at *all*. As we mentioned in an earlier chapter, as Jesus said in John 4:37, *"One sows...another reaps."* All God asks from us is that we are faithful to our calling as evangelists, and seize every opportunity God places before us to share His Good News.

Regardless of who receives which divine reward from our Master, we need to remember that God claims a sovereign right to do what He wills in His own affairs. It is not for us to question His choice of laborers, nor how He chooses to grant unto them specific gifts and talents, nor how He chooses to give them their respective rewards. Because of who and what He is, He cannot act unfairly. With our finite understanding, we may question His ways. At the end, however, as the Divine Interpreter, He will make any seemingly inconsistency plain to us. Till then, let us rest in His word, "I will pay you whatever is right."

We should just be grateful and count it a privilege that God has even chosen us. He has given us a particular place in His Body. He has given us a particular gift or talent He wants us to use. He has granted unto us something He has not given anyone else. And all He asks is that we use what He has given us to the best of our ability to His honor and glory.

It does not matter when He calls you to go to work in His vineyard. Whether He calls you as a Christian early in life, at mid-life, or late in life, all He asks of you in whatever time He has allowed for you, is to just faithfully serve Him *during* that time. If you do, He will reward you abundantly.

The important truth to remember here is that no matter *when* we start out on this road of evangelism, we are to continue traveling it as long as God grants us the ability to do so. The road never ends. We travel this road for God's glory, and He will reward us according to His good pleasure.

It is unfortunate, however, that even while we are traveling such a wonderful road with such glorious and heart-touching experiences along the way, there are some who may be a little "put out" by the way God chooses to reward His faithful children. I say that, not only from experiencing it first hand, but also because of a rather interesting question the landowner asks the "grumblers" in this parable.

Jesus asks the question in verse 15, *"Are you envious because I am generous?"* Fortunately, there are not too many Christians—at least I don't *think* there are—who have the kind of attitude displayed by these workers in the parable. But there are a few. After all, we still have that sinful, envious nature within us. And because of that, we need to remember that God is always gracious.

Regardless of what may be thought of His generosity, regardless of how some may complain about how kind He is, He will always be good and gracious to His children. He will always be willing to bestow His grace upon everyone who calls unto Him and reaches out to Him. God reaches out to us in our time of need. He grants unto us His love, kindness, compassion, and understanding. He calls each of us to come follow Him and work in His vineyard. He will grant unto us the ability we need to perform the tasks He sets before us. Not everyone can do what someone else can do. We have each been placed in the Body of Christ, as it has pleased Him, to perform that particular function in that particular part of the Body; and God has given each of us the abilities and tools to perform that function. If we are having difficulty, all we have to do is ask the Lord for help and He has promised us He will provide us the help needed. He has told us in Luke 11:9-10, *"Ask and it will be given to you; seek and you will find; knock and the door will be opened to you. For everyone who asks receives; he who seeks finds; and to him who knocks, the door will be opened."*

In this parable Christ is saying that we are to fulfill the work entrusted to us, leaving the distribution of reward to Him. The Lord is just, gracious, and generous, and He will do what is right.

This parable also encourages us who have been called at the end of the age, or near the end of our lives, to be faithful, for we may graciously receive a reward equal to that received by those who were the first called to Christ as His laborers, and who endured so much suffering and even death for His name's sake.

As laborers, may we ever remember that *motive* gives character to service, and that acceptable service is determined not by *duration* but by its *spirit*.

Once we become Christians it is our responsibility—our duty by Christ's command—to tell others about Him and what He has done for us. We see that all too clearly in Luke 8:39 when Jesus healed a demon-possessed man. Jesus told the man, *"Return home and tell how much God has done for you."*

There is a vast world outside our walls filled with lost people traveling down a broad road of destruction which leads to eternal separation from God. There can never be too many witnesses to share the Good News with those all around us. Jesus is always needing more to fulfill His task He gave us. He stated in Luke 10:2, *"The harvest is plentiful, but the workers are few. Ask the Lord of the harvest, therefore, to send out workers into his harvest field."*

All around us men and women are dying in their sin hopelessly condemned to spend an eternity separated from a God who loves them, and helpless in their own abilities to escape that condemnation. Apart from the grace of God there is no hope for any of us. There is no chance for any of us to earn the favor of God.

The most popular definition of grace contains only two words: "unmerited favor." But we need to amplify that a bit. Grace is what God does for human beings which we do not deserve, cannot earn, and will never be able to repay. Awash in our sinfulness, helpless to change on our own, polluted to the core with no possibility of cleaning ourselves up, we cry out for grace. It is our only hope. Our sinful natures cannot be improved, altered, or removed. We came into this life sinful, and we continue on in a sinful state.

It is difficult for a lot of people to accept this truth, that we are truly as sinful as the Bible teaches, as we mentioned in chapter 4 when we discussed goodness. On the outside we look good, almost clean at times. We may even look better than our world has ever looked physically. But there is something deep within us that is depraved. It is our nature. That is why we cannot clean up our own act. That is why we cannot handle our own lust. That is why we cannot say no to certain temptations. That is why we become addicted to harmful habits. That is why we fight with each other and fight with God—even when we know we shouldn't. If we are going to gain control over sin, it must come from *outside* ourselves.

The deadliest killer in our society is not heart disease or cancer...it is depravity. Every last one of us has it. Every one of us suffers from its consequences. And to make matters even worse, we pass it on to each new generation.

Several years ago a very interesting and eye-opening statement was released by the Minnesota Crime Commission. It stated, "Every baby starts life as a little savage. He is completely selfish and self-centered. He wants what he wants when he wants it— his bottle, his mother's attention, his playmate's toy, his uncle's watch. Deny him these once, and he seethes with rage and aggressiveness, which would be murderous were he not so helpless. He is, in fact, dirty. He has no morals, no knowledge, no skills.

This means that all children—not just certain children—are born delinquent. If permitted to continue in the self-centered world of infancy, given free reign to his impulsive actions to satisfy his wants, every child would grow up a criminal—a thief, a killer, or a rapist."

Now, folks, that's reality. And if it is your tendency to ignore it, it still won't go away. If it is your tendency as a parent to ignore it, that root of depravity will come back to haunt you in your home. A permissive, think-only-about-the-bright-side-of-life philosophy will be ripped to shreds by problems of depravity if your child grows up without restraints, boundaries, and controls. In his classic story, Robert Louis Stevenson proved that not even a kind and professional Dr. Jekyll could remove the savage-like Mr. Hyde from his own life. Face it, the dark side is permanently connected to us.

Yes, there is hope for lost sinners but it is all of grace. Our only hope is Jesus Christ. Not Christ and the church. Not Christ and good deeds. Not Christ and sincerity. Not Christ and trying real hard. Not Christ and baptism, Christ and morality, or Christ and a good family. Only Jesus Christ! Anything else is deeds, and "deeds" spells trouble.

You may ask why I have belabored this point of depravity and salvation by grace at this point, a subject on which all of us, as witnesses, are essentially clear. The reason is that even though we, ourselves, may be clear on this, those to whom we witness may very likely not be. When we witness to others, we cannot treat the symptoms of this disease called sin, we need to attack the cause, which is the depraved, sinful nature of all persons, but we need to do so in a loving and caring way, not being judgmental nor condemnatory. As we have mentioned previously, a witness simply reports what he or she has seen and experienced. It doesn't have to be a sermon or dump truck load of information. Just a word at the right time

about the greatest Hope in all the world. As evangelists, we need to help lost persons realize that despite their hopeless separation from God, they can, by faith, be justified and made acceptable to God.

Being justified does *not* simply mean "just as if I'd never sinned," as some have suggested. That doesn't go far enough! Neither does it mean that God makes me righteous so that I never sin again. It means to be "declared righteous." Justification is the sovereign act of God whereby He declares righteous the believing sinner while he or she is still in his or her sinning state. He sees us in our need, hopelessly lost and unable to escape from the swamp of our sin. He sees us looking to Jesus Christ and trusting Him completely, by faith, to cleanse us from our sin. And though we come to Him with all of our needs and in all of our darkness, God says to us, "Declared righteous! Forgiven! Pardoned!" Because of us? No way! Because of what Christ accomplished on our behalf when He paid for our sins.

All of that is included in what it means to be "justified." I come to God in all my need. I am hopelessly lost, spiritually dead. And I present myself to Him, just as I am. I have nothing to give that would earn my way into restoration with Him. If I could, I would, but I can't. So the only way I can present myself to Him in my lost condition is by faith. Coming in recognition of my need, expressing faith in His Son who died for me. I understand that God sees me coming by faith and admitting my sinfulness. At that crucial moment, He declares me righteous.

Although we need not—and obviously would not—go into all that detail, I have taken the time to share it so we can know what it means to be accepted by God even in all our sinfulness, and we can share the beauty of God's love and grace with those whom we are trying to evangelize.

They need to know that God loves them and they can, indeed, be made acceptable to a holy and righteous God even in their sinful state, that there *is* hope for them.

All along this road of evangelism we will meet all different kinds of people with all different kinds of needs. But the one need that all of them have is their need for reconciliation to a righteous God who created them in His own image, who once had sweet fellowship with Him, but that fellowship has been broken because of their sin. God wants to restore that fellowship with them and that is why He sent His Son to sacrifice Himself for them. God wants to give this gift of salvation to everyone, and once it is given and we have received it, it can never be taken away from us. It is not a wage that we earn for anything we have done like we earn our paycheck. It is a gift! And God is no Indian giver, nor can we forfeit that gift because of something we have done or have failed to do. Stop and think about that before you are tempted to disagree.

Listen to Biblical logic here, not human reasoning. If you work for your salvation, then you can certainly lose it. And that would mean it is not a gift; it's what you have earned. We really confuse things when we try to turn a gift into a wage. Furthermore, just as no one can say how much work is enough to *earn* the gift of eternal life, no one can ever say how little work is enough to *lose* it. If God required His own Son to die for you, He will certainly see to it that you are kept and protected through the various challenges and times of turmoil. So be confident and trust in God's security, not your own faithfulness!

Salvation is simply a gift. It's simple, but it wasn't easy. It's free, but it wasn't cheap. It's yours, but it isn't automatic. You must receive it. And when you do, it is yours forever!

This is the wonderful, life-giving message of hope we have to share with lost persons everywhere. I cannot think of any better, more reassuring message we could ever have to deliver to dying sinners. To be honest with you, my dear reader, I cannot help but be emotionally moved when I think of how much God loved someone like me, so much so that He sent His only Son to pay the ultimate price for my salvation. I cannot fathom that kind of love. I have *two* sons, not just one, and I know in my heart I do not believe I could ever sacrifice even one of them for some of the lowest, depraved people in this world. But that is exactly what God did for us. How can we not be grateful to Him? How can we not be touched by such a sacrifice? How can we not be moved to the depths of our souls when we ponder such unselfish love? And, as evangelists, how can we not be excited and more than willing to share that Good News with others? God made the ultimate sacrifice, not because He had to, not because we deserved it, not because we asked for it, but simply because He loved us. No greater love can be found than this.

The great Christian song writer, John W. Peterson, wrote a great song about Christ's love, which became my own personal testimonial song, entitled, *"O Glorious Love,"* in which he wrote:

> "O glorious love of Christ my Lord divine
> That made Him stoop to save a soul like mine!
> Through all my days and then in heaven above,
> My song will silence never,
> I'll worship Him forever,
> And praise Him for His glorious love!"

How could we ever get tired of sharing that message with others? How could we not *want* to share it? Whether we see any visible results from our labors or not, why should it matter? We are delivering a great message about the greatest story ever told. We are bringing a message of hope and peace and salvation to a hopeless, troubled, and lost world of people who need *something—Someone—*to believe in. As witnesses to the saving power of Jesus Christ, we have been called into the greatest and most rewarding service imaginable, and we should be forever grateful to our Lord that He has placed us here.

I was attending a pastor's conference at a Southern Baptist Convention a number of years ago, and this particular speaker was making reference to our calling as preachers, and even though he was addressing preachers, I would like to take his comments and apply them to our calling as witnesses for Christ.

He made reference to a statement made by that great Bible scholar, B. H. Carroll, who said, "I magnify my office, oh God, as I get nearer home. I can say more truthfully every year I thank God that He put me in this office. I thank Him that He would not let me have any other; that He shut me up to this glorious work. And when I get home among the blessed, on the bank of everlasting deliverance, and look back toward time and all of its clouds, and sorrows, and pains, and privations, I expect to stand up and shout for joy that down there in the fog and the mist; down there in the dust and in the struggle, God let me be a [witness]. I magnify my office in life. I magnify it in death. I magnify it in heaven. I magnify it for the poor or rich, whether sick or well, whether strong or weak, anywhere, everywhere, among all people. Lord, God, I am glad that I am a [witness], that I am a [witness for] the glorious Gospel of Jesus Christ."

What an exciting and wondrous task Jesus gave us. We may never see the results of our labors in His vineyard. We may never know if our message ever penetrates the hearts of those to whom we are witnessing. We may never know if that message falls on deaf ears or takes root in good soil and brings forth a bountiful crop. But, my friends, God knows; and God sees. We may do the sowing. Someone else may do the watering. Someone else may do the reaping. But God is the One who gives the increase. Every faithful laborer in His vineyard will be rewarded according to His good will and His perfect timing. One may sow and another may reap, but God receives all the glory… and that's how it should be.

As I said in the first part of this chapter, one of the most moving examples of this was a story told at another pastor's conference at a Southern Baptist Convention several years ago. The superb preacher and Bible scholar, Francis Dixon, told the remarkable story of the snowball effect of just one person who took the time to share just a brief word about the Bible's message of salvation.

There was a young man named Peter, who was in the Royal Navy in Sydney, Australia. One day he was walking down George Street in Sydney, when out of nowhere came this little, old, white-haired man, who approached Peter and said, "Excuse me, sir, but I'd like to ask you a question. If you were to die today, where would you be in eternity? The Bible says it will either be in hell or heaven. One of the two. Think about it, would you please? That's all, sir. God bless you. Too-da-loo."

Peter said, "I never had a question like that asked of me before. When I came back to England, the first thing I did was to seek out a pastor, and I was converted to Christ."

Mr. Dixon was holding a revival in Peter's church, totally unaware of Peter's conversion experience. As a matter of fact, the preacher had never met Peter. There were about six members on the revival team. One of the men was a young man named Noel. He was asked to give his testimony. This is what he shared with the congregation: "I was in the Royal Navy in Sydney, Australia. One day I was walking down George Street in Sydney, when out of nowhere came this little, old, white-haired man. He said to me, 'Excuse me, sir, but I'd like to ask you a question. If you were to die today, where would you be in eternity? The Bible says it will either be in hell or heaven.

One of the two. Think about it, would you please? That's all, sir. God bless you. Too-da-loo.'"

Noel said that he had never thought about that before, and it really got him thinking. So he went to talk to a minister, and he became a Christian.

After hearing Noel, Peter jumped up from where he was sitting in the congregation and said, "You've got my testimony!"

When Francis Dixon was on a world tour speaking in Australia, he preached in a Baptist church in the city of Adelaide, and he told this story of these two men. While he was speaking, a man stood up and waved his hand. He said, "Sir, I'm another. I was walking down George Street in Sydney, Australia, when out of nowhere came this little, old, white-haired man...."

Francis Dixon went across Australia to the city of Perth and he shared this story again. When the service was over, a deacon came over and said, "Sir, I'm another. I was walking down George Street in Sydney, Australia..."

Francis Dixon was so impressed that he went back to his church and shared this with his people. When the service was over, a young lady came up to him and said, "Sir, I'm another..."

Not long after that, Mr. Dixon was asked to speak at Keswick, that tremendous conference in northern England where people gathered to hear what Christ wants to do for us. He shared this story again, and when the session was over, a man came over to him and said, "Sir, I'm another…"

Francis Dixon made another world tour and was in India, speaking to some missionaries. He was asked, "Would you address us on the theme of personal evangelism?" Soooo…he told the story of that little, old, white-haired man, a story which by now was gaining more momentum with each telling. When the meeting was over, a woman approached him and said, "Sir, I'm another…"

Later, he was in Jamaica and shared this *again*, and *again* a man said to him, "Sir, I'm another…"

Mr. Dixon made one more trip to Australia, and visited the city of Sydney. He said to himself, "I want to see that little old man."

He asked his Christian friend and host, "Do you know a little, old, white-haired man who used stand out on George Street and ask people this question…?"

His friend replied, "Oh, sure! He's Mr. Jenner. All of us know him. He's quite feeble now, and doesn't get out on the streets any longer. He doesn't see well."

Mr. Dixon asked him, "Could you take me to his house?"

"Surely," his friend answered.

So they went to the house of this little, old white-haired man.

Francis Dixon introduced himself and told that little, old white-haired man of all these people that came to Christ as a result of that one simple, little question he would ask.

The old man broke down and wept, and said, "Sir, this is the first time in my life I've ever known of *anybody* coming to Christ through my witness."

One sows, another reaps. God receives the glory, and God will reward.

As evangelists, we don't know how God will choose to use our witness. All He asks from us is that we are faithful in our calling, whatever it may be, wherever He may place us, for however long He chooses.

I have always believed that perhaps one of the reasons God does not fully reward us upon our death, but waits until the end of the age when all His children are gathered around His throne, is because our witness that we left behind—our legacy—is still bearing fruit. Just think of all the souls who are still coming to Christ because of the faithful witness of people like the apostles Paul, Peter, and John; because of the loving concern of men like Edward Kimball, Charles Spurgeon, and D.L. Moody; because of faithful missionaries who have sacrificed so much and poured out their lives on mission fields all across this world; because of the simple, but profound, testimonies of men like Mr. Jenner, Eddie and his brother, Charles. As faithful evangelists in the cause of Christ, our witness will never die. It will continue on, long after we have left this mortal world and have put on immortality in the glorious world to come which Jesus has promised to all His good and faithful servants.

This road of evangelism we travel never ends. There are no rest stops along the way where we can stop and take a break from this great and glorious task God has placed before us. There are no detours, there are no shortcuts, there are no dead ends. We are to continue on this journey Jesus commanded us to take, over two thousand years ago. And as the time draws near when no man can work, it is even more important to stay the course and never waiver to the left nor the right.

Not everyone can be a preacher, a pastor, or an Evangelist (in the professional sense of the word). But every Christian has a part in God's eternal plan and purpose in His vineyard. And every Christian should be able to tell another person how he or she can also become a Christian. If you can't, then I strongly urge you to pray and seek God's guidance and help to learn how. If you profess to be a Christian and others are aware of it, you never know if or when someone who is seeking the solution to his or her feeling of hopelessness and despair may ask you, like the Ethiopian eunuch asked Philip, "How *can* I [understand] unless someone explains it to me?" After all, how did *you* become a Christian?

Paul writes in Romans 10:14-15, *"How, then, can they call on the one they have not believed in? And how can they believe in the one of whom they have not heard? And how can they hear without someone* [witnessing] *to them? And how can they* [witness] *unless they are sent?"*

As Christians, we have all been sent by the express command of Jesus Christ. He has sent us into all parts of the world. That world encompasses our homes, our communities, our work places, our churches. Everywhere we look there are people who are lost and in need of the message we bring. Evangelism is anywhere you *want* to find it. Let's go looking.

As Christians, we are all called upon to go to work in our Lord's vineyard. He has a specific task for us to do, and He has given us the ability and gifts with which to do it. Are we being faithful and diligent?

It seems like we only started this journey a short time ago, and even though we have come to this juncture in our travels, we know that this road of evangelism still stretches out ahead of us as far as the eye can see. I do hope this journey has been as enjoyable for you as it has been for me.

EVANGELISM: A Road Less Traveled

Evangelism can be one of the most exciting and thrilling rides you will ever take, and unlike at the amusement park, this ride never has to end. You can keep riding over and over and over again. With Jesus Christ in the lead, and we as evangelists, *following* His lead, we can *"press on toward the goal to win the prize for which God has called* [us] *heavenward in Christ Jesus"* (Phil 3:14). Around every turn, at the crest of every hill, at every intersection, new adventures await you; embrace them and enjoy them. New opportunities present themselves to you; seize them and make the most of them. Be happy in your calling as an evangelist. Be excited with your opportunity to share your witness with others. Be joyful in your salvation. Keep traveling down this never-ending and awesome road of evangelism and

Continue to enjoy the ride.
God bless you always and in all ways.
John 3:30

AFTERWORD

As we have made this journey together, I do hope you have been encouraged to take up the mantel and join the ranks of thousands of Christians down through the centuries since the birth of the Church, who have stepped forward and accepted the marching orders of our Commander in Chief. From the time of the first Christian revival on the Day of Pentecost in the opening chapters of the book of Acts to this present day, Christians the world over have come to realize how exciting evangelism can be. They have experienced a joy unspeakable and full of glory, which comes as a result of seeing just one lost soul embrace Christ as Savior. At the same time, just as Jesus did, they have also experienced the heartbreak of seeing people walk away from the only hope for their eternal souls. And, yet, in the midst of that heartbreak, they, likewise, have felt the sustaining grace of God encouraging them to continue on down this road of evangelism.

We must remember that evangelism is a never-ending struggle against demonic powers and forces of satanic darkness. We will not always win every battle, but the war against evil will ultimately be won. As evangelists, we are soldiers in this ongoing war. We can become discouraged and disheartened, but our General, the mighty Son of God, continues to lead His soldiers into the thick of the battle, and with Him leading the charge, we *will* emerge from the fray victorious.

Jesus sent us into a rebellious, troubled, war-torn, lost, and, oftentimes, defiant world to bear witness to His saving power, to a decadent society of self-centered and self-satisfied people who don't want to hear our message. We may be met with rejection, ridicule, and doors slammed in our faces. But we do not have to feel that we have to face such opposition all alone. Jesus will always be there with us, encouraging us, leading us, and guiding us by His Holy Spirit. We do not have to face a world filled with disdain for us all by ourselves. He has promised to be with us to the end of the age.

Even though we will be confronted with many obstacles along this road of evangelism, the many joys we experience at the same time not only make it all worthwhile, but cause those difficult bumps in the road to just pale in comparison. Trust me, my friend, there is no greater satisfaction, as a Christian, than knowing we are doing our Master's will when we are witnessing to others about His glorious love; and there is no greater joy than seeing—or finding out later—some lost person has found Christ as Savior as a result of that witness. There is also a certain inner peace we receive when we know we have obeyed our Lord's command to go into all the world to be His witnesses. That world for you may never extend any farther than the walls of your own home, your hospital bed, your work area, or the boundaries of your own neighborhood. But it is the world into which Jesus wants you to go. Go, then, rejoicing in the task He has given you, bearing the message of Good News He brings to all people.

This road of evangelism is a never-ending road, and we are called upon to continually travel it as long as the Lord allows us to do so. We are to be faithful witnesses for Jesus Christ and His love which He demonstrated on Calvary's cross. Of all the roads we travel in our Christian experience, this road is less traveled by God's children than perhaps any other. Jesus said, *"The harvest is plentiful but the workers are few. Ask the Lord of the harvest, therefore, to send out workers into his harvest field."* (Matt. 9:37-38).

Perhaps you are one who needs to ask the Lord to send *you*. My dear Christian friend, evangelism is anywhere you want to find it. *"Open your eyes and look at the fields! They are ripe for harvest"* (John 4:35).

Thank you, my friends, for taking this journey with me.

G. S.

2 Thessalonians 3:16

WITNESSING HELPS

*I*n order to be effective as evangelists, obviously, we need to have some knowledge of the Bible, and be pretty familiar with its truths regarding the lostness of man; and this comes from continually studying this Great Book. And, of course, we need to know some pertinent Scripture verses which are necessary when walking someone through the plan of salvation, as well as a witnessing technique. Someone once said, "A witness for Christ needs A Testament, A Technique, and A Testimony." There are numerous techniques when it comes to evangelizing the lost, and I do not believe that anyone can say any one particular technique is ether the best or better than some others. It really depends on who is doing the witnessing, the type of person being witnessed to, and the particular circumstance which led up to the witnessing interview in the first place.

My purpose in writing these next several lines is not to espouse any certain technique, but to provide the reader with possible tools to aid in his or her evangelistic approach. It is the reader's prerogative to use them or not to use them. Some may be helpful, and some may not. Some may be found to be rather complicated and in-depth, and some may be considered rather simplistic. In either case, these are just some tools which have proven to be quite beneficial to me, personally, over the years, as well as to others.

There are some who feel more comfortable in sharing the Good News with others by means of a gospel tract—and there is nothing wrong with that—so I have offered a few examples of familiar tracts which I feel are very effective. Others choose to use Scripture verses exclusively in witnessing, and I certainly find no fault there either. I have always felt that the best commentary on the Bible is the Bible itself.

So, if the following suggestions can help make you more effective as evangelists, then my offering them to you has served its purpose. Four gospel tracts I have found to be most effective and pretty self explanatory are:

Steps To Peace With God, published by the Billy Graham Evangelistic Association, and can be ordered through that ministry or it is available in some Christian book stores.

How To Have A Full And Meaningful Life, published by LifeWay Church Resources, and can be ordered through the Southern Baptist Bookstore.

The Four Spiritual Laws, published by New Life Resources, which is the materials distribution ministry of Campus Crusade for Christ International, and can be ordered through their website, or it is possibly available in some Christian book stores.

Eternal Life, published by North American Mission Board, SBC; Alpharetta, Georgia,
and can be ordered through their website, www.namb.net/catalog.

This approach and these verses are what I used when witnessing to Eddie, mentioned in chapter 14. It is one my father shared with me early in my Christian life, and one I've used many times. I have this taped inside the front of all my Bibles and New Testaments:

1. All of us are sinners	Romans 3:23
2. Unbelievers are under condemnation	John 3:18
3. Yet God loved us	John 3:16
4. And Christ died for you	Romans 5:8
5. He is our only hope	Acts 4:12
6. Only by God's grace are we saved	Ephesians 2:8-9
7. Believe on Him	Acts 16:31
8. Confess Him	Romans 10:9-10
9. *Anyone* can be saved	Romans 10:13

10. Live for Him   Romans 12:1

11. The Great Contrast   Romans 6:23

A five-step approach to witnessing to others:

1. All men are lost.

Romans 3:23

Romans 6:23

2. Christ died for you.

1 Peter 3:18

3. You must repent.

Luke 13:3

4. You must believe.

Romans 10:9-10...and then pray with the person.

5. Assurance.

John 5:24

1 John 5:11-13

An approach using only the book of Romans:

The Roman Road

Romans 3:23

Romans 6:23

Romans 10:9

Romans 10:10

Romans 10:13

These are just a very few tools and Scripture verses one can use as evangelists, and I realize there are a countless number of other methods available to us such as Evangelism Explosion, CWT, and many others which the readers—as well as I—have utilized. But, of course, time and space prevents me from listing all of them. But I do hope these tools will be of help to you as you travel this road of evangelism. But, as we mentioned in our study, always remember that we can have all these verses, and more, at our disposal, but somewhere during the course of our witnessing interview, to be effective, we will need to share our own personal testimony:

1. My life before Christ.

2. How I realized I needed Christ.

3. How I became a Christian.

4. How Christ helps me in my daily life.

A Few Verses Of Assurance

(Our Eternal Security in Christ)

1. John 10:27-29

2. Romans 8:35-39

3. 1 John 5:11-13

4. John 5:24

5. Romans 5:1

6. John 3:15-16

7. Romans 8:1

8. Philippians 1:6

9. John 1:12

10. 1 John 4:4

11. John 6:37

12. John 6:47

13. Ephesians 1:13-14

14. Romans 11:29

15. 2 Timothy 1:12